ladybug Love

100 Chinese Adoption Match Day Stories

compiled and edited by

Kat Lamons & Trish Diggins

Ladybug Love: 100 Chinese Adoption Match Day Stories

Compiled and edited by
Kat LaMons & Trish Diggins

Cover photography by
Jim Moore, AikoPhoto

Originally published by
Velveteen Press, Littleton, Colorado
Revised Edition published by
Marcinson Press, Jacksonville, Florida

Ladybug Love: 100 Chinese Adoption Match Day Stories
© Copyright 2013 by Marcinson Press
Printed in the United States of America.

ISBN 978-0-9893732-0-3

Published by
Marcinson Press
11111-70 San Jose Blvd., Suite 136
Jacksonville, FL 32223 USA
http://www.marcinsonpress.com

Please visit our authors' blogs
http://www.katlamons.com & http://www.trishdiggins.com

Dedicated to families
and children everywhere.

Special thanks to Willie and Pete.
Without you, we wouldn't be us.

acknwledgements

Kat Lamons

Many thanks to the families that allowed me the honor of sharing in so many adoption journeys.

Eternal gratitude to Willie. Without your support, volunteerism, and sacrifices, I could never have helped others to find the joy that we have always known.

A very special thanks to Lily. There are not enough words, in any language, to adequately thank you for your continuing contributions to my life – personal as well as professional.

Trish Diggins

Special thanks to my adoptive and biological parents, without whom I'd not be who I am today.

Grateful thanks to my friends and family who have contributed your time, talents, and support to making this dream come true.

Overwhelming thanks to my husband and my daughter; you are the loves of my life. Thank you for your support, encouragement, love, and your willingness to settle for many dinners of hamburgers and macaroni and cheese during the production of this book. I love you more than I can say.

about the auth🐞RS

Kat LaMons has been a professional in education and adoption casework for more than 20 years. During her years with Chinese Children Adoption International (CCAI), Kat shared in the creation of thousands of families. Her tenure as Director of the Joyous Chinese Cultural School and Director of Florida Operations for CCAI further enabled her to participate in the development of those adoptive families.

Through her adoption casework, writing and speaking, Kat continues to provide guidance on the subject of adoption, and to enthusiastically express the depth of her gratitude to those who gave her the extraordinary opportunity to make a significant difference in their world.

Trish Diggins has been a design, branding and communications professional for nearly two decades. Along with her award-winning professional skills, she brings an insightful perspective to the adoption discussion. As both an adopted person and an adoptive parent, Trish has the somewhat rare experience of living the subject from the inside out and the outside in.

Through her adoption-related writing and speaking she hopes to create opportunities for conversation, education, and understanding for everyone involved with the adoption experience.

"Ladybug Love" is a sincere thank you to adoptive families everywhere. In gathering and publishing these stories, we hope to honor adoptive families, bring hope to those still in process, and preserve just a little of the magic from those moments when dreams of family came true.

table of contents

table of contents continued

Introduction

This edition of Ladybug Love covers more than a decade of Chinese adoptions, from the days when people waited for "the call" to today, where people now search for "the one" *and* wait for "the call."

These stories are full of the real and sometimes raw emotions of those who have ventured into the world of international adoption. They've endured invasion of privacy, mountains of paperwork, endless governmental bureaucracy, years of excruciating waiting, and frustration that often grows beyond the capacities of even the most serene disposition.

To those families who are still in process, we offer a bit of hope. Even the best agencies in the world (and Kat believes she was with the best) can provide only so much support. They can certainly help families deal with the process on an intellectual level, but nothing soothes hearts and souls like the reassurances of those who have successfully gone before.

We've edited as sparingly as possible, while keeping the heart and feel of the stories as they were submitted. Names in these stories are pseudonyms and identifying circumstances changed to provide anonymity for families and for the children who may one day read about themselves.

Regardless of the content of individual stories, whether they're from families or adoption agency staff, you will find each match day story ends in exactly the same manner – with absolute, life-altering joy!

Happy Mother's Day

The wait had slowed to a crawl, which meant that year after year was rolling by without our match. Some days, I could handle it just fine, other days, not so much. My spouse and I were part of a group of waiting families that got together monthly, but after about three years, we found we couldn't handle ourselves during the months of December and May. It was too difficult to face the two holidays without our children. Without an official announcement, we found ourselves just not making any arrangements for those two months.

It was sad. Really, really sad, because it affected the meetings the month before, too. That meant that four months – not just two – were tough on us. That's a third of every year!

Every once in a while, China would experience a little hiccup in the timeline. Sometimes, it meant a delay in matches coming, but on rare occasions, the agencies would get two rounds of matches within the same month! These were so exciting, but so very rare, that I never really considered that they might affect our personal timeline.

Our group met early in April, but no plans were made for May. Some of us were expecting our match the following month, but it would be long after the holiday, and the waiting was already excruciating enough. We didn't need any reminders of it being a few more weeks.

One day, at the very end of April, I was just trying to get through the day when the phone in my office rang. I was at the drafting table and considered just letting the call go to voicemail, but decided that wasn't very professional of me, so I hurried over to the phone.

Seeing the agency's number on the phone, I panicked for a split second, wondering if it could be "the call." Then I remembered – matches had come a couple of weeks before, so I settled myself down before answering. Maybe it was a "get ready for match" call, where they double-checked which number to call, what address to send the packet, that kind of thing.

"Hello," I answered, noticing that although I'd done the logical thinking with my brain, my stomach was still full of butterflies.

"Hi," said the agency representative, "This is your agency, and we have some really good news for you! We're looking at a picture of your daughter!"

My legs gave way. I tried to aim for my desk chair, which I completely missed, and ended up crashing on the floor with the phone.

I yelled, "Hello! Hello!" because I was afraid I had broken the phone.

"Um... are you okay?"

I started laughing and crying at the same time, and somehow managed to let her know I was okay. The wonderful voice at the other end of the line told me all about my child. She added she was emailing me a picture, and would stay on the line until I received it and opened the attachment. Only then did I realize I was still sitting on the floor!

I asked her to hold on while I got the phone back onto the desk and myself into my chair. When I could finally open my email, the darling picture was there, and I let the agency representative know. We talked for a few more minutes, and I thanked her for the call.

Even though it was a few days early, she ended the call with words that I will never forget because they touched me to my very soul.

"Happy Mother's Day!"

DOUBLE HAPPINESS

We knew matches were on the way. The day before our expected Match Day we didn't sleep much. We knew we were going to see a picture of our little girl for the very first time. We called our adoption agency's director and said we were planning to come to their office on Match Day, as we felt we needed to share this special moment with the people who helped make our dream come true. It puzzled us when the director said we'd need to sit down when we got there, but we shrugged it off.

True to our word, on Match Day my wife and I drove towards the agency office, still pondering the "sit down" comment. Finally I said to my wife, "Maybe we got twins!" We'd talked about the possibility and made the request in our China documents. We dreamed it would be true, but we knew in our hearts it was unlikely.

As we drove to the agency, my wife started checking the blogs to see if anyone had been matched with twins. We knew there were twins every once in a while, and once we had seen two sets of twins matched. We figured if nobody was reporting being matched with twins, maybe that was the reason for the "sit down" comment.

My wife was watching the blog posts almost the entire drive. When we were about 30 minutes away, she said someone posted they got twins, so our hopes for twins started to diminish. About 10 minutes later, another couple posted they were also matched with twins. At that point, we knew we had been matched with a wonderful little girl, but certainly not two. We started discussing that maybe the agency had people who had fainted at match time, so that was why we were going to need to sit down.

When we arrived, our director met us at the door and suggested we take our seats in the conference room. My wife and I and both assumed this was the way matches were presented. I set up my video camera to record the event and we sat down.

The director said we might need to change the name of our blog since the title included our to-be-daughter's first and middle names. At that point I actually started to wonder if we had been referred a boy! Two red folders were simultaneously placed on the table – one in front of me, one in front of my wife.

Somehow, I knew right then and there that I was the father of twin girls. I slammed my hand down on the table and shouted, "Twins!" My wife was in complete shock. We had convinced ourselves that twins were impossible – yet, here they were!

We did rename our blog "Double Happiness." We were given the very best Christmas present when we arrived home from China with our beautiful twins on Christmas Day.

Telling us to sit down on Match Day was probably a wise decision on our agency's part. I don't think there's been time to do that since!

Hollywood Ending

When I received my referral call I had to tell the agency that I wouldn't be home to receive the overnight package due to arrive the next day. Because I was going to be doing a voice-over on a sound stage in Hollywood, alternate arrangements were made so that the package could get through the studio's complicated security measures to me.

All day I waited anxiously for the arrival of the package. Finally, near the end of the day I took a break from work and called the agency. While I was on hold, they spoke with the delivery company, who announced that the driver had come to the studio, made it through security, but then couldn't locate the sound stage. He was already on his way back to the delivery company and he STILL HAD MY BABY'S PICTURE WITH HIM!

I screamed and cried, and the agency representative assured me she would find a way to fix it. She promised to call me back as quickly as possible.

What I didn't know was that she was already on the other line, climbing the ranks of the delivery company until she found somebody with the authority – and the heart – to force the driver to turn around.

She pulled off a miracle because shortly after that my package was delivered to the studio. I didn't receive it directly because I had returned to work, but eventually, I was called out of the sound stage and handed the package. When I saw my beautiful child for the first time, I immedi-

nto tears of joy. The person called the "mixer" on the sound
...ust have felt the entire workforce needed an explanation of my
behavior, because at that moment, he announced over the studio loudspeaker, "Hey, everybody, Katie just gave birth!"

With that, the workday pretty much ended. Now THAT's a true Hollywood ending!

Adorable

Five years, four months, sixteen days. When I look at those numbers, I'm shocked. If you had told us we would be willing to wait that long for a child I would have denied it with every fiber of my being. To be completely honest, we thought about quitting many times, but I would usually call the agency and some poor soul there would talk me down. I'd always decide that since there wasn't actually anything we had to do, it was fine to just leave the adoption open.

Somewhere along the way, one of the agency workers explained to me that it was not unusual that I was looking at the special needs children. Our dossier was sitting in the traditional line waiting its turn. If we chose a child from the special needs kids, then the agency would tell China, and they'd get our dossier and match it up with the special needs child.

My heart went out to the little faces I saw, but I knew with our active family I couldn't choose a child that wouldn't be able to handle our lifestyle. Our kid would have to be tough and naturally active.

One day, my husband pointed out a little boy online. He was just so adorable. The special need was club feet. I told my husband this was not something I thought we should consider since it would mean surgery or maybe multiple surgeries.

My husband didn't agree. There was something about this little boy. My husband was drawn to him in a way he hadn't been with the little girls I'd shown him.

It turned out his paperwork wasn't with our agency. I knew that could cause a big hassle, but I went ahead and asked about the child's documentation and set up a round of file examinations with a couple of pediatricians and an international adoption specialist doctor. All the reports came back fine, so we decided we would go for this little man.

Our agency seemed hesitant about being able to get the file from the agency that had it, but said they would try. In the end, our agency and China convinced the other agency to release the file.

The day came when it was time to send over our request to adopt this child. I remember feeling a little confused. All this time, I had a picture in my head of a daughter-to-be, and now I needed to prepare for a son. My husband asked me one last time if I was okay with a son. I told him that I was, but inside I still wasn't all that sure.

The wait for travel was unbearable, but we got through it. The best day was when the agency asked us to give our child's new name. My husband and I realized that we had chosen a girl's name, but never got around to choosing a boy's name. We decided each of us would write down first and middle names on a piece of paper. When we showed them to each other, it was the same name! Our son is now named after both his grandfathers.

Less than a year after our son came home, we began the process for our daughter. As I write this, we are once again waiting for travel. Unlike the first time, we're calm and okay with the wait. We know what happens at the end!

Fall Festival

I was in the high school principal's office as I held the receiver to my ear. I felt weak as my husband whispered urgently on the other end of the line.

"I got a call from the agency! She said she just received a photograph! This looks like IT! Did you actually finish the paperwork?"

I had. It was late October and the Fall Festival was in full swing at our small country school. The festival was a major fundraising event for the school and everyone was involved – students, parents and teachers. The event was a huge competition between the K-12 classes to see which class could raise the most money for the school, with the winning class getting a day off. Being a teacher and a sponsor for the seventh grade class, I was busy cooking for the fundraising supper. I would also be involved in the carnival that night. We had high hopes of winning. The students had been selling raffle tickets and supper tickets all week, and frankly, we were all exhausted.

This was just one event among many that made my life as a teacher interesting. I worked part-time as a teacher and part-time as a freelance artist – which was like having two full-time jobs. My husband was the environmental coordinator for a large tire company, and had previously worked as a middle school science teacher. We were busy people, and we filled our lives with our careers and working with children. We chaperoned church and school field trips, volunteered to do talks for the scouts, and presented special programs for various school groups. We took students on camping trips and mountain climbing, taught children's groups at church, and I taught private art lessons for years.

Happily married for almost 20 years, we had a nice home and good jobs. We were a happy couple with a full life, but in our 40's with no children of our own. I'd thought about adoption, but had never really seriously considered it. Too much red tape.

Secretly, I had the desire to help orphans, but I didn't know how to go about adopting in our area. Then one day, while working at my drawing table, an international adoption announcement came on the radio. My heart heard the ad as it spoke of the need to place children from China in loving homes. So began my adoption research.

After much prayer, I was convinced the feeling wasn't indigestion. I felt like it was a good time to let my husband in on it. I approached him with something subtle like, "I feel we should adopt a child from China."

After I picked him up off the floor (well, not literally) we discussed it. To say the least, he was a little taken aback and hesitant to adopt any child, domestic or international. He put up some very good arguments.

Later, we went to an international adoption meeting focusing on China. We asked many questions, took copious notes, and came home with a stuffed panda bear and a mountain of paperwork to fill out.

My husband never told me not to fill out the paperwork. He always signed the forms when his signature was needed, saying all the while, "I'm just not sure this is the right thing to do." It was an arduous process, and after years of the paper pregnancy, the phone call finally came – to my husband!

There are instances in our lives where time seems to stop, or at least move in slow motion. I was standing in the school office with students swarming about in the rush of a busy school day with the added chaos of the Fall Festival. Yet, the world seemed to be moving in slow motion.

"How does she look?" I finally asked.

"She's a rather determined looking little thing! I'll send an email as soon as I can. I guess your really did send off the paperwork!"

The seventh graders didn't win the Fall Festival's top honor that day, but their teacher won something far more precious. My husband later wondered why he even questioned the decision to adopt. Our lives are now filled with even greater joy and blessings. And my husband is very happy that I finished the paperwork!

An invisible red thread

connects those who

are destined to meet,

regardless of time,

place, or circumstances.

The thread may stretch

or tangle, but it will

never break.

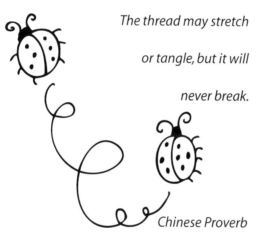

Chinese Proverb

Always and Forever

You know how people ask how you decided to adopt from China? I didn't know the answer to that question, because for as long as I can remember I've always wanted to adopt from China. My mother told me that the first time she remembers me talking about it, I was in junior high. So I have no idea where the idea first came from, but God pressed it upon my heart early, and it had remained there all of my life.

When we started the adoption process, I knew my husband was a little reluctant. It showed enough that our social worker really grilled him on his motivation. He explained that it wasn't that he didn't want to adopt, it was that he wanted both a biological child and an adopted child. The social worker seemed satisfied with his explanation, but under the surface I was still a little worried.

We prayed about it. My husband talked to some good friends who had already adopted from China. At some point, he seemed to come to a kind of peace about the whole thing. Then our agency sent us a file on a little girl with a cleft lip and palate. This was one of the conditions we'd marked as okay on our conditions list, but there was something about seeing the cleft for real. We weren't just talking in the abstract now. We took the file to our local cleft team to get their assessment, because that's what the agency told us to do. Once we understood the kinds of operations, the number of operations, and the likely years of speech therapy, I knew the reality would be too much for my husband. I waited for him to tell me no.

Because of the time limit we had to lock in the file, I knew we would have the conversation within a day or so. This would help me deal with the sadness I was feeling. I didn't mind the work that would go along with this child's special needs. I didn't mind dealing with multiple surgeries, even though I was scared to death. I didn't even mind committing to what could be years of speech therapy appointments. But my first obligation was to my husband. I knew he had to be comfortable with the decision.

The time for returning the file grew nearer. I was getting upset because I began to worry that my husband, so shocked by the pictures in the file, was going to say he didn't want to go with a special needs child at all. We'd barely spoken since we met with the cleft team. This was my husband's usual way of handling stressful situations. He needed time and space to process and then he would come to me with his thoughts. I was trying to be patient, but we were running out of time!

On the morning the agency told us the file had to be returned or accepted, I went to my husband. Unsuccessfully trying to hold back tears, I told him I would call the agency and tell them to release the file. I was surprised when he asked if that was what I wanted to do. Of course it wasn't! He explained he spent the day before not at his office, but running around talking to parents of adopted kids, talking with the cleft team again, and meeting with other specialists.

Long story short… he felt he had all the information he needed and he was ready to go forward with this tiny little treasure, but only if I was. He explained that he knew the majority of the workload would fall on me, so he'd been worried that I wondered if it might be too much. Me! The one who had always wanted to adopt! Me! The one who spent yesterday crying for a child that I'd never even met, but knew was meant to be mine forever!

Our precious girl is home now. She's had two of the three surgeries needed and her speech is vastly improved. It's been hard some days.

Not that hard, though… we're in process again!

I'm a Believer

My husband, Nathan, and I had been through the fertility wars. Worse, we'd almost completed a domestic adoption, only to have it rescinded three weeks before finalization. The day I had to give my son back to his birth mother was the worst day of my life, and it took me several years to recover.

It was really my husband who handled our international adoption process. In the beginning, I only agreed to it because I didn't want him to think I wasn't moving forward. I signed the necessary papers, accepted the intrusion of another home study, and waited to see if this one would stick.

During the entire process, I never spoke with anyone from our agency. We were able to designate a primary contact, so any time there were questions or something to be dealt with, they called my husband, or he called them. I was pretty much out of the loop, and I preferred it that way. It was my way of keeping myself from getting my hopes up.

The day before our referral call, our caller ID indicated the agency had called the house. I ignored it, since they hadn't left a message. I thought maybe they'd accidentally phoned the house then decided to call Nathan at his office.

The next afternoon, when I saw Nathan's car pull into the driveway about lunchtime, I didn't think too much of it. His office is less than five miles from home, so he occasionally drops by for lunch. I could tell something was different by the way he came through the back door yelling my name.

At the time, he didn't sound excited to me. He sounded scared. I immediately thought something was terribly wrong. I was afraid something had happened to our parents or his sister. When I saw the tears in his eyes I knew my world was about to change and I willed myself to remain calm.

It was obvious he was in no condition to speak. Without uttering a sound, he handed me the yellow file folder he'd been carrying. I stared at the unopened folder then back at his face. The tears weren't brimming in his eyes anymore, they were streaming down both cheeks! I hadn't seen that man cry since the day we married nearly 20 years earlier. It scared me to death to see it now.

Our adoption was the last thing on my mind. I took a deep breath, closed my eyes for a moment, then opened the folder. I found myself looking directly into the eyes of the fiercest looking little girl I had ever seen. In a single instant, I fell wholly and completely in love.

Nathan finally found his voice. "She's ours!" he said through a strange combination of laughter and tears, "The agency called me with the match yesterday, but I made them double-check everything for us again last night. Really, truly, we're going to get her in about six weeks."

I laughed. I cried. I kissed my husband. I shared the news. I prepared her room. I did everything a new mom was supposed to do. Secretly I never allowed myself to believe our dream would come true. It had been snatched away from me at the last minute before. As much as I dreaded it, I thought that was exactly what would happen again.

Belief would come incrementally. I came around a little as we boarded the plane for China. I dared to hope once I held her in my arms. I actually celebrated when we returned to the United States.

I'm not sure when the exact moment was that I became a true believer. It might have been the first time I tucked her into her own bed. It might have been the day we got her state birth certificate, or the day we received her American passport. Whenever it was, there's no question that I became a believer... enough so that we're now in process for another child.

This time, Mommy is the designated contact for the referral call!

When you drink the

water, remember

the spring.

Chinese Proverb

ME & MY GIRL

A lot of things can happen when you're waiting for your dream come true for more than half a decade. When we started the adoption process we were starry-eyed and hopeful, but after more than seven years passed, things were vastly different.

I don't know if it was the strain of the wait or other problems that were simmering below the surface, but about year six of our long wait our marriage fell apart. We tried to save it. We prayed. We treated each other with kindness and respect. We went to counseling.

It was in counseling that my husband, Michael, finally admitted that even though he had said he was okay with adopting, in his heart it was not something he wanted to do. The words he said were knives being driven through my very soul. I was the one with the infertility issues. I was the one that had originally sought adoption as a way to grow our family. I was the one who would now go forward, divorced and childless for the rest of my life.

Even after we filed for divorce, I did not tell the agency right away. I kind of thought that until it was final, there wasn't anything to tell. I realize now that I was just rationalizing. I was hoping to avoid the inevitable endings to the marriage and the adoption. A deep depression set in.

On the day the divorce papers were signed, I allowed myself an entire day of grieving. I didn't answer the phone. I didn't get on the computer.

I sat around in my pajamas and mourned my losses. I didn't think it was the right day to phone the agency, so I waited.

About a week later, I knew it was time to call the agency. I remembered something about any big life changes having to be reported to the agency and to the United States Citizens and Immigration Services. Not that I was concerned with the rules at that point. I was too miserable to care.

I reluctantly called the agency and asked to speak to my usual contact. She wasn't in, so they forwarded me to a woman I'd never spoken with before. She listened to my sad little tale, then said something that changed the course of the rest of my life. Even though I was now single, as long as I continued to meet the qualifications on my own, I could choose to continue with an adoption!

There was a new mountain of paperwork to finish, but I was able to qualify. A few months after that phone call my newly updated documents arrived in China. A few months later, I received the call I had waited for all those years!

I allowed myself an entire day of joy. I didn't answer the phone. I'm sure anyone looking in that day would have thought I'd lost it. There I was, dancing around in my pajamas holding a picture of my girl.

Me and my girl. It's been that way ever since.

"M" means Male... Right?

Sitting at a restaurant not too far from work, we were having lunch and talking about how we had all the time in the world to finish our nursery. We weren't expecting our referral for at least another couple of months. We had lots of other friends who were expecting their referrals that day or the next, but we didn't think we'd be getting "the call" for a while.

When I returned to my desk, I had a voicemail and an email with those infamous words, "You have a referral!" There was a brief description of her name and how she was doing in the orphanage, but no city or province.

Since I had a very important meeting I asked Stewart, my husband, to call the agency and get all the warm and fuzzy details about our little girl. We'd already chosen her name and we were so excited about meeting her that day – even if it was through a computer monitor.

The photo arrived that afternoon. So many people say this, but that child was more gorgeous than I ever imagined. There was one photo at five months, and several others taken more recently. With a May birthday, we were likely to just miss that first birthday celebration.

We looked at the photos over the weekend. On Friday, when we saw a translated copy of the letter from the China Center of Adoption Affairs we noticed the gender of the baby was listed as "M." Stewart mentioned this to the agency but they dismissed it, saying they received a lot of letters like that. This was most certainly a girl!

We had friends over for dinner. One of them kept telling us that we really needed to keep an open mind – after all, it did say "M" on the letter.

On Monday morning, I receive a call from the agency saying our baby was indeed a healthy baby BOY! It took me about three seconds to get over the fact that we would be meeting a little boy rather than a little girl.

Since we had two beautiful biological girls, and we hadn't specified a gender, it had always been in the back of my mind that the CCAA might see fit to send us one of their little boys. After all, he would be spoiled rotten with three "mothers" around him for the rest of his life!

When the agency representative began explaining about the mix up, she told me that they could arrange for a new referral of a girl in about four weeks time.

"Oh, no! That's my baby!" I emphatically assured her. I could tell she was not expecting that reaction at all!

WISHfUL ThInKIng

The flurry of activity associated with the paper chase ended quite suddenly in January. Now it was time for us to wait quietly for months before we'd receive the call informing us about our daughter... who she was, where she was, and when she would be ours forever.

The next months passed quietly, spring turned to summer, summer into fall. We heard about friends receiving "the call." When the group of waiting parents in front of us finally received their calls, we knew we would be hearing in another few weeks. We were next!

Both of us stayed home that day to finish up work and projects. The fall chill in the morning air was refreshing as we went about our work. My wife, Marlena, studied for a securities test, while I worked on the honey-do and other lists of things to be done before travelling to China. We were not expecting "the call" until at least a week later.

The phone rings. I wondered who would be calling on the home line. We usually got calls on our two business lines. Maybe my nervous mother, who thought it'd be this week, and she just wants to chat. Maybe it's Marlena's work looking for answers or approvals. Maybe... just maybe... it's "the call!"

"Hello... hello... hello?" I listen intently for a human voice... but no one is there. Hanging up, I stare out the window. Wishing, wishing, wishing it had been "the call!" Today is Friday and there's plenty to do, but here I stand, wishing and thinking and praying the phone will ring since we're both home. Then I remind myself next week will be fine since Marlena will get the call first at her office.

The phone rings again.

"Hello, is this Gordon?" the voice says. I've spoken with our agency representative many times. I know her voice quite well.

"Yes! Do you have good news?"

"I DO have good news!" she says, and I can actually hear the grin in her voice.

"WAIT!" I cough out. Trying to keep calm, I manage to get a choked-up shout to Marlena. "PICK UP THE PHONE!"

The questions disappear in tears of joy. We simply want to enjoy this moment.

"Fax me the papers and overnight me everything! I've got an email already started. We'll check with a doctor and a specialist…"

"Slow down," our happy stork commands. "We've got a lot to get through!"

We receive more information and pictures. Within hours, the combination of phone lines and call waiting enable us to have up to six people on the phone at the same time.

We are parents! Our parents are first-time grandparents! And in traditional Chinese style, all sorts of people become aunts and uncles.

For us this means the end of a lifelong wait and the beginning of life anew.

Dazed and Delighted

When we decided to embark upon yet another international adoption journey, we were pretty comfortable about how the process would go. After all, we'd already been to not one, but two foreign countries. We were old pros, and though we would never have publicly admitted it to others, we did harbor a little feeling of superiority.

We didn't allow ourselves to get stressed over the timelines or rumors from China. We didn't sign on to any Internet lists or join any support groups. We were already members of our local Families with Children From China, and we felt that was enough.

Even with the advent of September 11th, we were confident that adoptions would continue, just as they had through all other international crises. We might have done a little more checking than usual, but honestly, we didn't get too worried.

The adoption process timeline for our first child had been less than six months. It'd been about a year for our second child. That we were looking at well over a year this time seemed just a part of the natural order of things.

Of course, we still paid attention to correspondence from the agency. I called the update line once in a while and every so often the agency would call me to clarify a issue or remind me of a due date. Overall, we didn't feel like there was too much to get excited about. We knew the timeline. We were prepared to settle in for a long wait. I guess you could say we were more than a little laid back during our third round.

On the day of our referral call I'd been out shopping for most of the day, youngest daughter in tow. My older daughter was in an after-school program that afternoon, so there really wasn't any hurry to get home. We dawdled in the department stores and I even let my daughter play in the toy store for better than half an hour.

When we got home our voicemail was beeping. I walked to the phone and was flabbergasted to find not two or three, but eleven messages! I don't know why, but instead of listening to voicemail, I checked caller ID.

I didn't recognize the agency number or the abbreviated version of their company name, but I saw that someone had left four messages. What shocked me more was seeing that my husband's office had called seven times!

I didn't think my husband had ever called home that many times in a single day. I was pretty worried. It was just a few minutes after 5 p.m., so I tried his office. Just as I picked up the phone, he pulled into the driveway. I ran out the front door only to find him sitting in the car, head down on the steering wheel. Now I was really worried.

He must have seen me out of the corner of his eye. He raised his head and stared straight at me wearing the craziest grin I'd ever seen coupled with a look of shock. I didn't know whether to laugh or cry, but I was going to find out what was going on right then and there!

As I approached the car, he reached over and locked the car doors. I was stunned. He leaned over, grabbed something off the seat and pressed it against the window. It was a huge picture of a darling baby. He peeked over the top of the picture, eyes crinkled with laughter, as I tried desperately to get the door open.

The moment I realized it was our match I came completely unglued. All that calm, all those months of control disappeared into the afternoon sky. I started banging on the window, shaking my fist at him, laughing and crying at the same time. I was carrying on like a fool and he just sat there laughing through his own tears. It seemed like forever before he was out of the car hugging me and giving me the information about our daughter!

We were both dazed and delighted. "The call" not only went to Dad instead of Mom, it had come early!

Make happy those

who are near, and

those who are far

will come.

Chinese Proverb

Those Eyes

For almost the entire adoption process, my wife, Heather, was the one who filled out the forms and talked to the agency. Heather was the one online with hundreds of people who were suddenly our friends and with whom she shared way too much of our story. Heather was the one who expected to find our child, too.

I thought China just took your information and they picked a baby for you. I was surprised but happy when my wife let me know that when you are okay with special needs you get to pick the child. I knew we had a list in with our agency and they were looking for a child that fit our criteria, but it seemed like Heather was always on the computer looking at a lot of different websites with pictures of the available children.

I didn't give it a lot of thought. I figured my input would start about the time we were travelling to China. Oh, I had plans in my head. I was going to be the best dad there could ever be. I was going to make sure that little girl, whoever she was, would turn out to be a daddy's girl.

Once in a while, Heather would show me a picture and we would request more information on the child, but it never worked out. We always found that the child had a special need that was outside of our capabilities. Don't get me wrong, we came into the process knowing that we would adopt a special needs child. It's just that we live in a rural area, so special needs that would need weekly trips to doctors or ongoing medical attention just wasn't in the cards.

One night Heather had the laptop in the bed and was browsing more sites. She would ooh and aaah at kids here and there, but she didn't bother interrupting my TV show for any of them. When my show ended, I peeked over her shoulder and saw a row of children's pictures. The second from the right was of a child, obviously malnourished, with eyes that melted my heart. I tried to be casual as I asked about her.

"She's got extra digits," she said, but it was such a strange thing to hear that I didn't comprehend what it meant.

"What else?" I asked.

"Looks like they think she was premature, and she has delayed development."

"Of course she has delayed development, she was a preemie!" I thundered, as from seemingly nowhere, the papa bear in me came out.

Heather smiled at me with that knowing smile of hers. You men know the one. It's the one you've come to both love and hate over the years. At that moment, I knew if there was any way possible, that little princess would call me Daddy one day.

The Princess has been home for a couple years now. She's just about outgrown that "Daddy's Girl" shirt I bought her. No problem. Don't tell Heather, but I bought it in every size it came in. I think they'll last all the way to middle school.

POWER ON, POWER OFF

Our adoption agency had already informed us that we would be getting our match call that day, so it was no surprise that we woke up to a perfect morning. I'd been out of state with our biggest customer on a fishing outing. My husband was home with our two biological daughters, getting them ready for daycare. Everyone was SO excited!

As my fellow co-workers and I approached the city, the sky was growing darker and darker. By the time we reached the office around noon it was apparent my beautiful morning was giving way to one ugly day.

No real worries, though. This was the day of "the call" and nothing could bring me down. My excitement even affected my co-workers. No amount of rain could dampen our spirits on this day! Back at work, I tried catching up on mail and email, but I found it very hard to concentrate. I jumped each time the phone rang. Co-workers kept popping in to see if I'd heard anything. Finally, around 3 p.m., a co-worker who'd become a very good friend stopped by. We were both so anxious.

I signed on to our agency's online group to see if there was any chatter and… there was! I started trembling, knowing that at any minute the phone was going to ring.

Within one minute….

R-r-r-r-r-ing!

The receptionist announced she had the adoption agency on the line. I just smiled at my friend and said "THANK YOU!" Then, I took the call

I'd been waiting to receive for so very, very long.

I was very nervous, but started writing down everything I was being told in a fairly legible fashion. Suddenly, the unthinkable happened.

The power went out.

I screamed, "NOOOOOOO!" followed by total silence.

Everyone within earshot heard me, knew what call I'd been on, and instinctively knew not to come within range of me. I found my cell phone, called my husband, Rich, and talked as fast as possible.

"I-was-on-the-phone-with-Dana-at-the-agency-and-the-power-just-went-out-so-I'm-sure-as-soon-as-she-realizes-she-can't-get-back-in-touch-with-me-she'll-call-you-unfortunately-the-agency's-phone-number-is-in-my-computer-which-I-can't-turn-on-so-get-on-the-Inter-net-and-look-it-up-for-me-quickly-please!"

Rich found the number as quickly as he could. Before I knew it, I was reconnecting with the agency – just as the power came back on. I told the agency receptionist who I was and what had happened. She said Dana was on the line and she was certain she was trying to call me, could I please hold? Yep, Dana was trying to call. Could I please hang up?

R-r-r-r-ring. Dana couldn't believe the power went out during the call, either, and we attempted to pick up where we'd left off.

Of course, nothing in life is simple, and the power went out a second time! Immediately picking up my cell phone, I called the agency AGAIN, told the receptionist the story AGAIN, and finally – FINALLY – received the remainder of that long-awaited call!

ThIRd TIMe's the ChaRM

We had been waiting years for our baby from China. Like everybody else, we were more than a little discouraged. I brought up the possibility of moving to the special needs program. Two of my friends had started their adoptions at the same time we did and were already home. One of them had been home for two years.

We worked hard on the list of conditions that we were willing to consider. Like a lot of people, we wanted something that was relatively minor. We knew we didn't have the money or the time to deal with anything that required long-term medical treatment and the accompanying costs.

We were pretty excited upon receiving the first file from the agency. There were expectations that the child would have one of the minor conditions that we had listed. Once we started looking at the file, we began to understand there can be a broad range of severity under each condition. We told the agency that we really wanted minor versions of the special needs, so we were returning the file in the hopes somebody better equipped would be given a chance to raise the child. It sounded good. It sounded logical. But I felt like my heart had a little piece torn from it the day we refused the file.

We were also scared that maybe, because we'd turned down a child, we wouldn't be given another chance. We were scared that our file would go to the bottom of the list. We were really happy and surprised when another file was sent to us only a few weeks later!

Both of us read through the file, and though the special need was a little more than what we had originally thought, we felt we could possibly handle it. Our agency insisted that we take the file to a doctor to examine, but we didn't really know anyone local. The agency gave us some names of doctors that specifically worked with international adoption families to examine files, and we contacted one.

It turned out that the special needs that we were concerned about were not that big of a deal. The doctor recommended several specialists not too far from us, and then lowered the boom. There was something in the exam indicating the child had a far worse condition than the special need we were discussing and they recommended against the adoption.

We were devastated. My husband told me that it was more than we should have to bear, to fall for not one but two children only to realize that it was not meant to be. We alternated between being angry and being sad for two days, and then we told the agency we were turning down the second file. The staff was polite and they said they understood, but it was obvious they were concerned maybe we weren't really open to special needs. One staff member suggested that we meet with our social worker and really work through the list and our perceptions. It was hard to take because we knew we were committed to a special needs adoption. We just needed to be realistic about what we could and could not handle.

Several months passed. I was secretly convinced that we were being punished for that second refusal, but the agency assured me that wasn't the case. They told me that finding minor special needs just took more time. I tried to accept that and went on with my life.

One day the phone rang. It was my favorite agency representative, the same one that had been reassuring me about the minor special needs. She was obviously excited and hurriedly told me they had found the perfect child for us. I thanked her for the call and anxiously waited for the file to come through in email.

When we opened the file, it had a picture of a darling little girl. She was breathtakingly pretty, with dark eyes and a very full head of hair. The file said she had a minor heart condition that had already been repaired in China.

She was, and is, perfect for us.

The journey of a

thousand miles starts

with one step.

Chinese Proverb

The Best Laid Plans

Both of us had been married before. I did not have any children from my first marriage, but my husband had four daughters. That may have been why he was reluctant to sign on with a Chinese adoption program.

"But, you've got all this experience," I reasoned with him, "and you'll be able to teach me whatever I need to know." I don't know if he fell for my line of reasoning or what, but eventually Darrin said we could go ahead with the adoption process. And so the paper chase began without my having the slightest understanding of how excruciating the wait could be.

I think I must have become pretty unbearable. I noticed we were seeing less and less of our friends. I found that Darrin and I seemed pretty testy with each other. Even my favorite agency representative once told me that I had to find a way to calm myself. She gently told me that it would do my future daughter no good to be delivered into the hands of a mother that had driven herself insane! The months came and went. And came and went. And came and went.

Sometimes I felt like my mind went with them. When "the call" finally came and I was informed that she was a he, I was certain my mind really had slipped away during the incessant wait!

"No, you really have a boy," Susan explained, "and he is unbelievably cute! Are you okay with a boy? Your home study didn't designate a girl or a boy."

"My home study didn't what?" The jargon of the adoption process held no meaning for me now, "and did you really just tell me for SURE that it's a boy?"

"It's a BOY!" she answered loudly as if sheer volume would get through to my brain. It took a while, but I did finally absorb all the information. Then I called Darrin – the father of four girls – and announced that he had a son!

The Forgotten Client

It's a morning like any other. I am up at 5 a.m. checking email. I scan half a dozen lists and hundreds of messages looking for that magic word: REFERRAL. At 7:20, I reluctantly shut down the computer, shower, and dress for work. When I get there I find a ladybug pin left for me by a co-worker. I put it on. My workday begins.

At 11:30 a.m., I begin a meeting with a client. Two minutes later, my co-workers Donna and Lisa appear in my doorway. They are red-faced, grinning widely and quivering. "You have to get the phone!" they shout.

I dart from the conference room to my office and blindly reach for the phone. I know this is "the call!" These days, I routinely burst into tears as I wonder obsessively about my soon-to-be-daughter. Who is she? Where is she? What is she doing today? Is she having a good day? How old is she?

"Hello?" I squeak out.

"You have a daughter," says Tracey, from my agency. I'm sobbing and can't speak.

"Are you okay?" she asks several times. I finally recover enough to make a noise, so she continues with my daughter's name, birth date and province. She patiently repeats herself as I tightly clutch my pencil and try to force my trembling fingers to form the letters she is spelling out. Donna and Lisa are hopping around and peeking over my shoulder, trying to see what I am slowly managing to transcribe.

We hang up, then I remember I need to request that they send my referral picture by email so I call the agency right back.

I get voicemail and leave a message. Lisa later confesses she was going to call the agency back and leave a second message because she was pretty sure nobody there would be able to decipher words so choked with emotion.

I call my parents.

"Hello?" It's my Dad. I try to speak.

"Uh, um, uhm a ma ma ma!" bursting into happy tears again. I'm reduced to a low whine.

"Who is it? Hello?" My dad adjusts his hearing aid. By now, my mom is on the other phone.

"Hello!"

"You're grandparents!" I finally blurt out, then tearfully relay what little I know about their new granddaughter.

It's now 11:43 a.m., and I remember my abandoned client. He's been told what's going on, and just kisses me on the cheek, saying he'll call to reschedule the appointment. I know it sounds odd, but I had dreamed that I'd be with this client when I got "the call."

I phone the agency again. They're laughing and saying they were just listening to my message. I've settled down enough to start asking my many prepared questions. Luckily, I had these ready beforehand, because my brain obviously stopped working when I got "the call!"

We wait by the computer screen until finally, at 12:05 p.m., a message pops up.

"You have a message. Would you like to read it now?"

We couldn't hit "yes" fast enough.

A click of the button is all it takes and there, at long last, is my perfect, beautiful daughter!

lifetime story

We had put in our checklist, so the agency already knew the special needs that we were interested in. We'd been told the wait would be about a year. That seemed okay to us, but the year came and went. When we asked about the timing, we were told that it would most likely be a few more months because they weren't seeing the special needs we had asked for as often as they had in the past. We were disappointed, but what was a few more months? We were aware of many folks that had been in the adoption process for years, so if we were able to complete our adoption in less than two years, it still seemed very reasonable.

While we were waiting, we tried to squeeze in all the "couples only" activities that we could. We went on two cruises. We spent a week at a dude ranch. We even took ballroom dance lessons. With all that activity, you would think the waiting would not be a burden, but it was. It was always there, just under the surface, and it bothered me a lot.

About 16 months into our process, I decided we had waited long enough. I started scouring the adoption websites in order to find a child. I knew my agency would not be happy if I found a child with another agency. I was more concerned about giving a child a home, so I decided to go for it. Every morning, I would get up a half hour early, fix a cup of coffee, then sit down with my computer. It became a ritual.

All the pictures were so cute, but as I read the information on each child, I began to realize that a lot of the special needs were more involved than I thought. I came to the conclusion that we had turned in our list before we were ready. We really had not studied the medical conditions enough and had no real concept of the kind of care that would be needed. I decided to talk with my husband about our checklist and to suggest that we pull out – at least temporarily. The plan was that I would speak to him over the weekend when neither of us had any work pressure.

On Friday morning, the phone rang. It was the agency asking if we would like to see a file that they felt fit well within the parameters of what we had said would be acceptable. I was hesitant at first, considering my plans for the weekend, but I told them to go ahead and send it.

My husband arrived home just as I was going through the file. When I told him I thought we needed to talk, he immediately assumed I meant I wanted to talk about the file. He grabbed the paperwork from me and started reading it out loud before I had a chance to say anything.

As he read, his voice began to get a little shaky. By the time he finished, both of us had tears running down our cheeks. We stood there staring at each other, both of us apparently coming to the same conclusion at the same time.

It really didn't matter what her special need was. This was a child destined for us, and we were destined for her. We both knew it in our hearts from the moment he began reading that day.

A Shocking Situation

So there I was, practically shouting my praises about this beautiful child. But I was getting nothing back from the new mommy on the other end of the line. I was genuinely surprised! This was a woman who had cried when she received the news that her dossier had been logged in at the China Center of Adoption Affairs. This was a woman who had checked in with me, her adoption caseworker, weekly for almost a year.

Yet, she had become eerily quiet once I announced that this was "the call." I finally asked her if she was okay. "Uh huh," came her quiet, hesitant reply.

"Elizabeth, are you sure? Should I go back through the information with you?" I was growing genuinely concerned.

"Uh uh. I have to go now," and with that, she hung up. I was flabbergasted!

I was fairly certain she hadn't taken in the information, much less written it down. I wondered if I should call her back. I wondered if I should call her husband. I decided to trek into the boss's office for a little advice, but I was interrupted by a call coming in. I scurried back to my office and picked up the phone.

"YOU'RE HAVING MY BABY!" said a booming male voice. Now it was my turn to be speechless! He must have realized what he said, because he immediately attempted to correct himself. "No, I mean MY WIFE SAID YOU HAD MY BABY!" He was getting closer, but it was still a little off.

I couldn't help myself. I broke into a fit of giggles. It was more than a few moments before I stopped guffawing long enough to ask to whom I was speaking! The man, of course, turned out to be Elizabeth's husband, Dave. Although she had managed to make the phone call to him, she really had gone into a complete state of shock, and had not retained a single bit of the information I had given her!

Dave later told me that Elizabeth had remained in shock until he arrived home with the pictures that I had emailed to his office. It was the picture that finally made the whole thing real for her. It made me very glad that "we have the technology!"

sudden Realization

There were all kinds of stories out there. We were older parents, adopting for the first time. Our agency said that because of our ages, we were likely to receive a child at least 18 months old. Still, I clung to the stories where older parents miraculously received very young children.

My mind accepted what I was told, my mouth even repeated the words back to the agency representative and our social worker. But my heart… well, that was another matter. Even though I knew better than to share it with anyone else, including my husband, Tom, I knew I wanted a baby.

Like a lot of other people, we got into the program just as the huge slowdowns began. This was a real worry for me, because every month that went by meant we were a month older. I thought that would affect the age of the child we were matched with. I secretly stewed and fretted, but kept a thin veneer of calm on the outside.

"She's 14 months old," was the answer to the only question I bothered to ask during the referral call. I didn't receive the news very well, but somehow managed to get through the call without falling completely to pieces. We both knew I wasn't ecstatic, but nothing was said.

Once I hung up the phone I simply sat in my room and cried. Gone were my dreams of the "mommyhood experience." Gone was my desire to continue with this adoption!

This was back in the days before agencies began to email the children's pictures. That meant the official information wouldn't arrive until the next day. Since Tom was out of town I decided not to call him with the news just then.

The package arrived in what must have been the earliest of the deliveries in our town. I took the single photograph out of the package and set it on the breakfast table. I had to admit that she was cute and she appeared so, so very tiny. (Of course, that could have been due to the miniscule size of the picture!)

I stared at the picture for hours. Finally, I decided I had better let Tom know the "good news." I tried to call him, but no luck. I couldn't locate him. I hadn't heard the phone ring earlier, but he had left me a message, saying he was flying home that evening instead of the next morning. I would have to share the news in person and I was dreading it.

When the phone rang in the late afternoon, I half expected it to be Tom, but it was our agency, instead. They were calling to report bad news. Our daughter was seriously ill. There was the possibility that she would not survive. They would make arrangements for another match just as quickly as possible. They were so very sorry.

"Sorry? SORRY?" In that instant, I came to the sudden realization that they were talking about my daughter. She was no longer just the picture sitting on the table. That was MY DAUGHTER! Her age was no longer of any concern at all to me. I just needed her to make it until her parents could come to get her.

"You've got to help her," I sobbed into the phone, "and tell them we'll pay for whatever it takes! Do whatever it takes. Just don't let her die. PLEASE don't let her die!"

Tom arrived home to find me a complete wreck. That was the way things remained for nearly a week. Then we received word that she was improving and we would be allowed to go through with the adoption, after all.

Until asked to tell my story for this book, I never told a soul – not even my husband – how I felt when I first received our referral. I have been too ashamed and too grateful, because we now have a beautiful, healthy child who is nothing less than the light of my life. I tell my story now in the hopes that it will help somebody else struggling with the age issue.

Of a small spark,

a great fire.

Chinese Proverb

panic pays off

On the day we received our referral, we'd already had quite a bit of excitement that morning – an electrical fire in our office! The whole place smelled pretty bad.

We were given the option to go home. I took it. Once I was home, I immediately got on the computer to see if any referrals had come in. There were families from my agency posting about receiving their referrals. Since we hadn't heard anything and it was now early afternoon, I was frantic. Somehow, I convinced myself that the China Center for Children's Welfare and Adoption had decided we would not be allowed to adopt, so in tears, I called the agency and asked to speak to Katie, my usual contact.

The receptionist explained that Katie was with a family and asked if she can take a message. At this point, I was sobbing. I told her I noticed referrals had come in and we should have been in this batch. She tried to calm me down, and asked to put me on hold to see what she could find out.

After what felt like hours, she got back on the phone and said yes, we do have a referral, and the agency was in the process of contacting all the families. Once again, she put me on hold to see if Katie can come to the phone. Suddenly, she's there, telling me about my daughter! I'm trying to write down all the information so that I can tell my husband, and she finally says, "Just get down here!"

I hang up and call my husband, but when I tell him that we have our referral he doesn't believe me. He thinks I'm kidding! I keep trying to convince him but he isn't buying it. Finally, I say I'll be right down to his office so we can go to the agency together.

That was the longest 10 minutes of my life! While I'm heading to his office, my husband calls the agency to get directions. I still think he was calling to see if we actually did get our referral, and to make sure that I hadn't gone off the deep end. When I get to his office, he's so excited he's shaking like a leaf.

We finally get on our way, and at the speed he was driving I was worried that we would get into an accident. Amazingly, we get to the agency in one piece, enter the conference room, and Katie presents us with the file.

I will never forget the moment we saw our daughter's picture for the first time. She was so beautiful, so sweet... we screamed and cried and laughed in delight! For so long, we'd dreamed about what she would look like, and now to finally see her face was wonderful and magical. Here was our daughter, and she was more beautiful than we could have ever imagined.

I guess we really can say we never did actually get "the call" because I called first in an absolute panic after I'd convinced myself it was never going to happen for us. Once we received our referral, the feelings of joy and gratitude went way beyond mere words.

Our dream finally came true, and it touched a place inside of us so deeply, we have never been the same.

Baby Bok Choy

In the middle of our adoption process, we decided to retreat to the mountains where there happened to be a well-known children's outlet store. Taking full advantage, I had a few hundred dollars worth of clothing and accessories in various sizes and for various seasons draped over my arm. I must admit that my husband, Greg, is the sensible one in the family. He talked me into putting everything back except for one package of washcloths. Greg went outside while I went to the cash register. I carried the washcloths to the front and on the way picked up one little pink dress. I couldn't resist it – and it was just one!

During our wait, we referred to our little girl as Baby Bok Choy. Our friends and family were anxious to know what we were going to name her. We had several names picked out and once we settled on one, we decided to keep it to ourselves until we got the referral. So, Baby Bok Choy it was.

Out of town on a business trip, I checked in with Greg late one evening. He told me our agency director had called to be sure one of us could be home the next day around noon to receive a package from a courier. Greg wasn't exactly sure what they were sending to us. Both of us assumed it was more papers to sign. I was very discouraged. This would hold up everything!

I was to leave for home the next evening, but decided to catch the morning flight instead. I was nervous.

I was seated next to a squirming two-year-old boy. Would I ever have the opportunity for my own squirming child? My eyes filled with tears many times during the flight. Once we landed, I went to the nearest phone to see if my husband had the mysterious package yet. I wondered if he was as upset as I was, but then I reminded myself that Greg was the sensible one.

When he answered the phone, he immediately asked me if I was sitting down. "Of course not. I am in the middle of the airport. What's the problem?" I said in exasperation.

"I'm glad you didn't paint the nursery pink," he said.

"What? What do you mean?" Suddenly, Mr. Sensibility was making no sense!

"We have a boy!" I could hear the grin in his voice. "We have a son! It's a little boy, and he's only few months old!"

"How do you know? Is he okay? Why do you think it's a boy? A BOY? That's not possible. This is China, how could it be a boy?" I was finally interrupted.

"His picture is right here."

"But how do you know it's a boy?"

"It says so on the form and there's a picture of him!"

"But –"

"The picture is in split pants, and he is a boy in all his glory! It really is a boy! Baby Bok Choy is Baby BOY Choy!"

I got my luggage and hurried to the car. I cried the entire 40 minutes it took to get home. A little boy! Was he really okay? Was this a mistake? I had always wanted a little boy but we were adopting from China, and everyone knew only little girls came home from China. I had to see for myself.

The picture took my breath away. He was, indeed, a boy. With the picture was a note from the agency. It read, "Just a minor explanation. For Chinese, having a boy is very proud thing. One way to show proud (sic) is to show HE IS A BOY, as the picture shows. Hope you understand."

We immediately called the agency to accept the referral. The lady on the other end asked if we knew what we wanted to name her. I said, "Her is a him, and we have no idea! Right now, he's just Baby Boy Choy."

Needless to say, when we met the other families in our group on the way to China, we were the only parents without an 8" x 10" enlargement of their referral picture. We were also the only ones bringing home a boy. And thanks to my sensible husband, there was only one dress in the closet!

Govern a family as you

would handle a small

fish – very gently.

Chinese Proverb

Guess Again

Part of our job as agency staff is to help families keep their expectations as realistic as possible. As the China adoption timeline became longer and longer, it was more and more difficult for us to accomplish this. Everybody, including staff, was becoming pretty disheartened. It just seemed to be cruel and unusual punishment to even suggest to parents that the end result of this long and difficult journey might be only a grayed-out variation of a dream-come-true, as it was often difficult to keep hope and excitement sustained for an adoption that would take years and years to complete.

We had one particular family that was a bit older, but had requested a healthy girl, 0-12 months of age. We knew this was everybody's dream, but we felt obligated to gently remind these parents-to-be that it was highly unusual for a young child to go to older couples. Every time we spoke, I tried to steer the conversation to how much larger an 18-month-old was than a 12-month-old; how a walking child was going to take more energy; that a child nearing two would likely have some distinct personality traits already well-developed, and such. My hope was that these little doses of reality would soften the blow for the couple once they received a match more in line with their age qualifications.

On the morning of Match Day, the couple knew from the Internet rumors that matches would be done that day. They called to say they were driving the few hours down to the office since they wanted to receive their match in person. We were thrilled to have them come in, because Match Day is a high for us, just as it is for the families. At first nobody said it out loud, but we were also more than a little worried. It was going to be harder on our hearts to actually have to see the disappointment in person.

We began preparing matches for the day. Since there were several, we did not get to this particular family's match right away. When we did we were completely dumbfounded to learn that the couple had been matched with a 10-month-old. They would likely be sharing her first birthday with her!

We did a little more decorating for this couple than usual. We talked about all the time we'd spent trying to prepare them for acceptance of an 18-to-24 month old. We listened with excitement for the telltale sign of the agency door opening.

When the family arrived, we ushered them into the conference room where a red file folder lay upon the table. As they sat down they asked if the folder contained a picture. We said it did.

When everyone was seated, we opened the file and the first thing they saw was the face of this glorious child. We had taken the tiny passport size photo that accompanied matches and had blown it up on our color printer so they could get a good look at their little darling.

The staff could barely contain our excitement as it was, but when the father exclaimed that she didn't look very old, we just couldn't hold back any more.

"*She's 10 months old!*" we shouted together.

I'm not sure who smiled first or who got teary-eyed first, but my memory of the next few minutes is a room full of people all grinning like fools with tears running down their cheeks. It had been a while since we had shared a dream-come-true. That day reconfirmed the staff's faith in miracles and reconfirmed a family's belief that dreams really do come true.

MY DAUGHTER, YOUR DAUGHTER

I had been a nervous wreck all weekend. When Monday finally came, I knew referrals were coming. I went to work as usual, but I didn't get much done because every few minutes I kept checking the Internet for referral notices. Some were posted, but none from my agency.

The day dragged on. By mid-afternoon, I figured I'd have to wait another day. Then… there it was! A referral posted online for my agency. Forget work! I was so nervous and excited I couldn't function on even the most basic level.

A few minutes later the phone on my desk rang, and thinking it was the referral call, I answered. I wasn't thinking straight. I answered with the name of my adoption agency instead of my company. Luckily it was a coworker, who was kind enough to keep my temporary insanity under wraps.

Just before quitting time I got "the call." Her province was Gansu. I'd never heard of anyone traveling to that province, so it was pretty exciting. She was 15 months old – perfectly within the age range I'd requested. Amazing!

After a few minutes, composure regained, I remembered to ask my agency representative if she'd gotten her own referral. I knew she was expecting a referral about the same time I was. She had! Although I was really excited for her, I was trying to remember all the things I should be asking about my own referral.

"So, what does she look like?"

"Well, she has a cleft lip and palate..."

This totally threw me, because I'd requested a healthy child, and here she was describing this medical condition in a pretty matter-of-fact manner.

"What? I was expecting a healthy child!"

"Oh, sorry, I thought you were asking me about my daughter!"

We laughed. I felt a little relieved and a lot stupid. She told me my photo had been emailed. A few seconds later, I was looking into the face of my new daughter for the very first time. She was sporting a bright green sequined vest and seemed to have quite a head of hair. Her outfit seemed surreal, as had the entire conversation, and, well, pretty much the entire day. It was a day I'll never, ever forget.

That Voice

The years kept rolling by. I was in my thirties when I started the adoption process, and now I was nearing middle age. Some days I was angry. Some days I was sad. Some days I just felt foolish for hanging on to a dream that was obviously never going to come true.

While I waited, my sister married. She had a first child. She had a second child. I was happy for her, but it hurt every time we visited. How could it be that I had been married for 15 years and was still without a child, while she had been married for only five years and had two children? The unfairness of it all hit me hard, but I kept it inside because I wanted to be a good person. I wanted to share in my sister's joy. I wanted to be reasonable.

Inside, I was slowly going crazy. It was a functional crazy. I still worked, still took care of my husband, still kept our home nice, but I would find myself daydreaming. I would find that 10 minutes had passed while I stood with the dish sponge in my hand. I would wake up in the night thinking I had heard a child's cry. After a while, the weeks and months and years became a blur underscored always by the emptiness and longing in me.

At first, I was in a lot of groups online. Sometimes this was helpful. Sometimes, it was so painful I ended up signing off for a while. After the first few years, I gave up on the groups. It was just too hard to act as if I was okay when I wasn't. I stopped following the occasional email from the agency. I decided if God wanted me to have this child, He would let me know some day, some way. In order to survive, I just put the whole adoption out of my mind and heart as much as I could. We updated whenever the agency told us to, but did nothing more.

One afternoon several years into the process, I absentmindedly picked up the phone when it rang. I recognized the voice, but just couldn't place it. When the woman on the other end of the phone told me it was "the call" I was momentarily stunned. Then all the years of pent up emotion burst out and I start sobbing uncontrollably. The poor woman on the other end of the phone had to patiently wait until I calmed down.

Of course, all my plans for the match call were out the window. I had long ago thrown away my list of questions. I forgot to have the agency do a telephone conference to include my husband. I didn't even have the presence of mind to open my laptop.

The voice seemed to be coming from some far away tunnel. It was telling me that a picture of my daughter had just been sent to my email. The voice was waiting on the line to make sure I got it.

Time slowed to a crawl. I can still remember the feel of the edge of the computer as I pushed the screen upright. It took me four tries to input my computer password. I remember seeing the mini version of the email on the left side of the screen, but couldn't remember how to open the email or the attachment.

The voice asked if I could see a little paperclip logo either on the top of the message, or in the body of the email. I could see it, but couldn't figure out how to open it. The voice instructed me to just click on it, then click on the paperclip. I know how to use mail and download files. It was unreal that I forgot how to do all that, but when I clicked the paperclip, my daughter's beautiful face filled the screen and I was reduced to a puddle of sobs again.

To have the depth of my sorrow replaced with the height of my joy by a voice in phone call was pretty spectacular. It was nothing compared to what I now experience every single day of my life!

A Patient's Patience

With this being our fifth child, I guess it was only appropriate her daddy got "the call." At the time, I couldn't believe he got the news first!

Initially, the agency had tried to call me on the home phone. To this day, I don't understand why I never heard the phone. They also tried my cell phone. It was on, but it had been left in the car. Finally, they decided to go ahead and call my husband, Garrett, at his office.

A physician, he was actually with a patient when he was summoned from the room to take the long-awaited call. As he learned the information, there was no way anyone within hearing distance could have missed the news! I still can't believe that his entire office, including his one very patient patient, heard everything before I did!

The agency was emailing the picture of our daughter to our home, not to his office. As soon as he hung up, Garrett called me at home and shared her orphanage name, birthday, and the name of the province she was coming from. He told me to check our email for a picture of our newest daughter!

Needless to say, the entire family rushed to the computer – three brothers, one sister, and one Mommy. I was crying. The kids were jumping all over the place, asking why was I crying!

We forwarded the picture back to Daddy's office, where he proceeded to show her off to absolutely everyone. Even his abandoned patient had waited to see her picture!

Love and attention

make all things grow.

Chinese Proverb

Times Two

I remember being confused by the news that China would now allow families to adopt two children at a time, or successively, or something! I didn't understand how the new system would work, so I called our agency.

The staff at our agency all know us because it's a very small office, so even though the person I wanted to speak with wasn't in, I was able to talk comfortably with another staff member. She explained the new system to me. It all made such perfect sense. After waiting all these years, we would be able to create an instant family! We were going to adopt two at once *as soon as I could convince my husband of the plan.*

He didn't appear overly enthused. He was full of questions, though. How could we afford two kids at once? Was that even good for the kids? How could we deal with two separate sets of special needs at the same time? What about the logistics of just getting two kids from two different places in China? How could you adopt in two different places at once? What about the logistics of getting two kids on several airplanes between China and home?

I have known this man most of my life. The speed of the questions being volleyed at me was a clear indication that he was genuinely considering taking this crazy action. I answered as much as I could, but suggested that we do a conference call with the agency so he could hear things first hand. We set up a time for the conference, and naturally, he ended up working overtime that day. We had to reschedule. That happened twice more before we finally got on a call together with the agency.

Once we thoroughly understood the process, both of us were committed to completing all the steps necessary to go forward with two adoptions. What this meant was that I had to do everything and my husband just signed on the dotted line whenever he was asked. It wasn't that difficult, but as the time passed I grew more and more concerned about what we might be getting ourselves into.

We are an older couple. We've never had kids. We are a little bit set in our ways. I was not at all confident that I had the energy to handle two children at once. I almost spoke up, but just when I was at my lowest point the miracle happened. We were offered a file on a child that would suit our family perfectly.

Because the agency knew we were interested in two, within a few weeks we found our second child. Their special needs were pronounced, but repairable. It looked like there would be a lot of medical visits and bills in the beginning, but the hope was that it would end once the initial work was done.

We have been home for more than a year now. The first few months were very hard, but I wouldn't change anything. We have our child "times two" and we are so blessed.

We LIED... A Little

After waiting for several years for our regular match to come through, we did what a lot of people decided to do. We moved over to the special needs program.

And we lied. A little. We sat in our family room and told our new social worker – our first one had moved away and our second one quit – that we had actually been open to special needs all along.

The truth was that we had never been against a child with special needs. We just hadn't considered it because it wasn't necessary to consider back when we started. People were getting healthy children from China all the time. The process was relatively painless and relatively fast. We just happened to enter it at about the time the great slowdown started.

Going over the special needs conditions was a real education for us. What we thought we would be open to turned out to be far more involved than we thought, while other conditions that sounded too complicated turned out to be well within our ability to handle. We did our homework. We talked to families. We spoke with some specialists. We even attended a couple international medicine meetings.

We turned in our list and waited. And waited. And waited. When another year passed, we felt like something was really wrong. Either our agency wasn't actively looking for a child for us, or our expectations were unrealistic, or... something. We called the one staff member we knew and asked if she could look into the situation. She told us that it wasn't her area, but she could at least make some inquiries.

Just a few days later, we were sent a file. We were ecstatic. That is, until we had our specialists look at the file. The condition was not minor as we had thought. The doctors recommended against the adoption and we were heartbroken. When we told the agency we would not be able to accept, they were very kind and reassured us that the child would be adopted by the parents that were just right for her. I so wanted to believe what they told me.

A few more weeks passed before we were sent another file. I was a little afraid to open it for fear of the disappointment I had already experienced. I was just about over that first file, but it had taken some time and a lot of tears. I didn't want to start down that path again. I had my husband download the file and give me the information without letting me see the picture. I thought this would protect me from falling in love again.

The condition didn't sound too serious, but it wasn't anything we had studied in depth, so we needed to get some extra help with assessment – really fast. I didn't know where to turn, but the agency gave me the names of some international adoption doctors. We emailed the file to one of them, explaining that we only had a day or so to lock in the file. We didn't hear anything back that day.

The next morning my brother-in-law mentioned that he knew a specialist for the condition and kindly called him for us. This man, a stranger to us, took the time to look at the file and talk to us. It was an unexpected blessing. We hung up the phone feeling that we would most likely adopt the child. Just then, my cell phone rang and it was the international adoption specialist. I spoke for another 20 minutes with this doctor, but my husband had disappeared from the scene.

Now we had it confirmed by two different specialists that we should go through with the adoption of this precious child and I still hadn't seen her picture! I hollered for my husband, but there was no answer. I looked through the entire house, but he was nowhere to be found. Finally, I hit the garage. There he was, sitting in my car. He had printed off pictures of our little girl. She was smiling at me from the back seat windows, and a smaller version was hanging from my rearview mirror. I drove to work that day with my daughter – a scene that has repeated itself many times in the two years since she's been home.

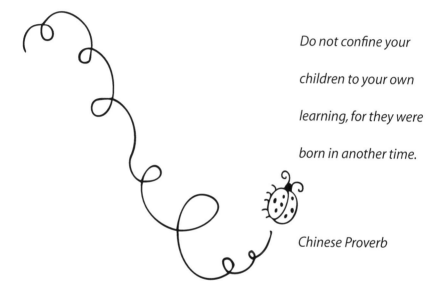

Do not confine your

children to your own

learning, for they were

born in another time.

Chinese Proverb

MULTI-TASKING

When I called my agency on Monday to check on referrals, I was told the referrals were in the mail. To me, this meant I should expect "the call" to come on Friday – perfect timing after the long wait.

I picked up the phone the next afternoon and it was my agency representative calling me to tell me I had a baby girl. She told me my daughter's name, age, and which orphanage my little girl would be coming from. Shaking and near tears, I remained in shock as I listened to the details about my baby. I couldn't believe it! We had a baby and she was located in the province of Guangdong. That was an answer to my husband's prayers.

The representative, who was actually looking at the picture of my daughter, described her to me as a big girl with cute, chubby cheeks. She wanted to know if I wanted her picture emailed to me. Of course I did! I gave her my home email, which I told her I couldn't access from work. She laughed.

"We are quite advanced here, you know," she giggled, "and we do pretty well with multi-tasking. I can send the picture to more than one email address at a time. Would you like me to send it to your work email since that's where you are right now?"

The shock must have been wearing off a little by then, because I finally agreed to have her email both addresses. We discussed a few more details, then hung up, so that I could give the news to my husband.

I immediately called him. "We have a baby!" I shouted. We stayed on the phone for a while as I gave him all the details. Unlike me, he wanted to wait until he got home to see her picture.

I began to wander aimlessly around the office, telling some of my co-workers that I was now a mommy. I also explained her picture was being emailed to me. Everyone must have realized what a complete daze I was in. There I was, walking around the office while her picture was sitting in my email! Several of the group rushed me back to my desk.

My first glimpse of my baby wasn't shared with my husband, but with some of the other people who had also waited with me during the years. Everyone was so very excited about this little girl halfway around the world.

One of my co-workers printed her picture out for me on the color printer, so we would all have her picture with us from that moment forward. She continues to be a well-loved baby by all those I work with, not to mention by her adoring mommy and daddy!

Happy Together

When we submitted our dossier, we requested a child that was slightly older and a little more independent. When we received "the call" we were elated to learn our daughter was nearing her second birthday. We were also given some other basic information – and then the agency representative offered to email her picture. But she warned us that our little one must have had her shots right before the picture was taken, because she most certainly did not look happy.

Wow! When the picture came through, unhappy didn't come close. A deeply furrowed little brow and a wild buzz haircut with an expression that looked like she had just swallowed a few sour lemons. It took me a while to take it all in. The next day our package arrived with some additional pictures, and there she was again with a less-than-thrilled countenance. The packet said she was starting to walk and she was moody if she didn't get her way. She seemed like a typical two-year-old, and we said yes!

It was a while before we travelled to China, and thankfully we received a few updated pictures where she didn't look quite so unhappy. She wasn't smiling, but she wasn't miserable, and she was definitely cute. That was the photo I printed out and carried around with me. I also asked the agency to please follow up and request that her caregivers continue to work on her walking and to please, please not cut her hair again!

The day we met our daughter, she walked into the room. Her hair was starting to grow out, and she was actually smiling. We saw the return of that furrowed brow a few times during the adoption trip (and to be honest, more than few times after we got home) but now she is a happy, healthy girl who wakes up with a smile!

The Pact

Our story is a little different. My husband, my 10-year-old biological son and I had made a pact with each other that we'd all be there together when we saw our baby girl's face for the first time.

We saw online that some parents had received their referral, so we knew sometime that day we'd get "the call." It was a snow day, so my son and I were home, but my husband, Jason, was working.

The phone rang non-stop all day. Every time it rang, my son would run through the house and grab whatever phone extension he was near. My mom, my dad, my grandmother, my sister, my brother, our friends, our neighbors, my husband all called at least a dozen times, every time asking, "Have they called yet?" *No, but if you don't stop calling we won't be able to get "the call!"*

About 2 p.m., it rings again. My son runs and slips and slides across the kitchen, right into our beloved blind shih tzu, sending them both sprawling across the floor. Even so, he's the one who sees the caller ID.

"Here she is, Mom! It's our Jade!" he screams. He's so excited, he forgets to even say hello and blurts out, "Do you have my baby sister?"

"Yes, I do have your baby sister, and she is something!" says the angelic voice on the other end of the line.

Suddenly this burly, never-cries little boy, who would rather run over a quarterback or throw a baseball than breathe, has tears streaming down his cheeks. He proudly boasts to the voice on the other end that he will be the first one to hold his baby sister in China. Finally, he hands the phone to me. I'm crying so hard I can barely understand anything more than her name, age, and where she's waiting for us.

We hang up and immediately call Daddy to tell him to hurry home as quickly as he can. At that moment, my son and I are co-conspirators. We know that on the computer on my desk is the face of his baby sister, the daughter I've been waiting years to see. We circle like two vultures, looking at each other, trying to read each other's thoughts.

Could he be thinking what I'm thinking? Does Jason ever have to know? Couldn't this be one of those precious mother/son secrets that we carry to our grave? Can we survive the 20-minute wait for Jason to drive home from the office? In these few minutes, I think back to two years earlier, sitting in front of this very computer, showing my son what his baby sister might look like as we browsed through the online pictures of that year's referrals.

"Mom, when will I see my Jade?" His question was part of our private discussions. He could never say this stuff in front of his friends. He had an image to maintain! This was something we shared, just the two of us, late at night. Dreaming of our baby girl. So, since we'd shared – just the two of us – so many times, would it be a such a stretch to "accidentally" see our Jade before Daddy got home?

I sat and watched as my son paced the floor until finally he blurted out, "Okay, Mom, I won't tell Daddy if you won't! We can act really surprised! I can't wait any longer!" He'd read my mind.

I snapped back to reality as I heard the door close. My husband came running in, once again sending our poor dog sprawling. I was so relieved we hadn't given in. We all three sat together in front of the screen, tears rolling down our faces and the picture rolled up. There she was – there was our Jade! The most beautiful baby girl we'd ever seen. We sat, holding hands, staring at this precious child, knowing at long last our family was complete. She was very much worth the wait.

My son will happily tell anyone who will listen that weeks later in China, he was, indeed, the first one to hold his baby sister in his arms.

Daddy Plans Ahead

I was driving to my husband's office when my cell phone rang. It was our adoption agency.

"Let me connect you to Dean," said the voice on the end of the line. Suddenly we had a conference call going. "I'm driving!" I shouted to them. I had just realized I was in my car! They both laughed and told me to pull over.

We had a healthy baby girl! We were given her name and its meaning. Her birth date turned out to be exactly 100 years after her great-grandmother's. Talk about a red thread!

We received a picture of our daughter at age three to four months. *She is beautiful! She is perfect!* We think she has Dean's hairline and my fair complexion. That's our baby, and we are totally in love with her! Her daddy falls asleep on the living room floor, her picture beside him. It's really sweet.

We drive over to my husband's parents' house with a bottle of champagne and pictures. They cry. They fall in love with her little picture immediately. This is their first granddaughter and they're very excited. They want her here. We want her here, too!

We go out for Chinese food, keeping her picture on the dinner table. We begin to think about what will happen in the next few weeks and months. It is a dream come true. Reality has not even come close to setting in yet.

Tomorrow the overnight package will arrive with more information, pictures, and paperwork. There will be consulate appointments and travel arrangements to deal with. Daddy has already begun working just a little ahead on that portion. He has booked us on 48 different flights between our "best guess" travel dates!

ARE YOU SURE?

In some cases, the decision to adopt a second child is made at the same time as the decision to adopt the first. That was my situation.

Several years ago, I knew I would be making a second trip to China right after my first. While I was prepared for an uncertain and extended timeline, my new superior at the high school where I was an assistant principal was not. He was pressuring me for more information. In response to his questions, even though I knew I was still a couple months away from my match date, I picked up the phone and called my agency.

When one of the agency directors answered, I explained that I understood I was still a couple months out, but I was hoping for any news I could relay to my boss. The agency representative got very quiet and said, "I need to check something. I'll be right back." Another five minutes passed before he picked up the phone and said, "So, you are a mama!"

I practically snarled at him. "I know I'm a mama, I want to know when you think I will get my match."

"No, you are a mama now!"

"I know that, I want to know about the match."

"I am looking at her and she is very cute," he explained, frustration now evident in his voice, "and she looks like me!"

It finally began to dawn on me – just what he was trying to say.

"Well, if she looks like you, then I don't want her!" I said.

"That's a joke, right?" asked the quiet voice on the other end.

I immediately revealed that of course it was, and told him I would drive up to see her picture and sign the acceptance as quickly as I could. When I hung up, I went absolutely wild in my office! My celebration was then tempered a bit by my assistant, who wanted to make sure that the agency truly had our match as I was the one who called them, not the other way around.

Her caution did make me wonder, so I called the agency back and spoke to another staff member. After a few minutes of double-checking, I was assured that I did, indeed, have a match and that the entire staff was waiting for me to come and see her picture. I immediately took off for the agency… and that special picture.

Ordinarily, the trip between my office and their office takes about an hour, but on that day it seemed to take almost no time before I was staring at a picture of a darling baby girl. Her special need was a congenital heart condition. She was far too tiny for her age, but she was mine, and I was determined to bring her home as soon as possible.

It would take antibiotics, hospital stays, love, and time to cure her, but she has now grown into a delightful, healthy, bright girl, and I am honored to be her mom!

Daddy Decorates

When we were in the adoption process, my job required a lot of travel. In spite of this, I devoted a lot of time to preparing our daughter's room. My husband, Jack, and I selected a crib that could convert to a toddler bed – just in case we ended up with an older child. We bought additional furniture, painted the room, added stuffed animals, and began a book collection that threatened to outgrow the space before the room's resident was even home!

As the anticipated time for our arrival grew nearer and nearer, so did my anxiety. It was hard to keep the agency informed of my whereabouts, since I was traveling every week. It would have been great to have a cell phone, but my boss had made it clear that he'd better never learn that a personal cell phone had interrupted a meeting with a client. That meant whenever I arrived at a new location, I had to call the agency with the hotel number, my room number and my meeting schedule. Although I couldn't take personal calls in meetings, messages could certainly be left. I always checked for them during breaks, lunch and dinner.

One Friday evening, after a grueling day of negotiations that had not gone well, I called home for a little spousal support. Jack knew what a difficult week I'd had, and I was looking forward to his soothing words and wise advice.

I was surprised to find that he wasn't home at dinner time, but I reasoned he was probably sick of his own cooking and had run out to get something to eat. I took a shower, ordered room service, and tried again. No answer. No answer an hour later, or two hours after that. I was tired and lonely. I was also getting irritated. I got ready for bed, then tried one last time.

On the very first ring, he answered, sounding very sleepy.

"Were you sleeping?" I said, "Are you sick? I've been trying to call you for hours!"

"No, I'm not sick. I was sleeping. It's midnight here, you know."

"But I've been trying to call since early this evening!"

"I spent the whole evening working in the garage, so that's probably why I didn't hear the phone."

His explanation was odd, both because there was a timbre to his voice that I didn't recognize, and because he isn't the kind of man who tinkers in the garage.

"What?" I was definitely questioning his response and his actions.

"I got to thinking about how we're going to need room for a stroller and a bike and…"

"Oh, for heaven's sake," I said, "Strollers fold up in the trunk of your car and she won't need a bike for years."

The conversation turned to the results of my meetings, his plans for the next morning and the specifics of where he'd pick me up at the airport the next afternoon. We said good night and hung up. I went to bed with a vague feeling of uneasiness.

When we arrived home from the airport the next day, I walked into my living room to find bouquets of flowers *everywhere*. With them, new pictures on the fireplace mantel. Pictures of our new daughter!

In the nursery, there was a new set of pictures on the dresser – one of Mommy, one of Daddy, and one of baby. In the kitchen, a photo of her on the microwave. Beside the bed, an enlargement of one of the photos from the mantel. He'd even placed a tiny picture of our new daughter on the edge of my bathtub!

Jack explained that he'd kept the referral call a secret because he wanted to be with me and see my face when I got the news. I never did figure out how the call went to him instead of me, but I forgave him for keeping the secret. I also complimented his decorating!

If you want

happiness for a

lifetime -

help the next

generation.

Chinese Proverb

Tea for Two

By the time our daughter reached her third birthday, we were absolutely amazed at how far she had come from the sickly baby we'd received in China. She could already recite the alphabet. She could count to 20. She could recognize some letters well enough to read them. And she knew that baby sisters came from... China!

We have never really been sure how she learned the baby sister part, but she knew it like she knew her own name. She was quite insistent that we begin doing whatever had to be done to get her little sister home.

We had always intended to adopt again, but planned to space our children just a little further apart, so we did what a lot of parents do – we tried to explain that it could take a very, very long time for a sister to arrive. Santa might have to come at least three more times before a baby sister would.

For her third birthday, our daughter asked for a baby sister. That Christmas, she asked again for a sister. She then wanted to know if the Easter Bunny could bring a sister. Finally, she took her grandfather aside at his birthday, and asked him to wish for a sister for her when he blew out the candles.

We'd been out of the international adoption loop for a while and didn't realize that the waiting times had really changed. We had received our first match in less than six months and we were shocked and disappointed to learn that it would take about three times that before we received our second referral. It looked like the spacing of children would be on our original plan, not our daughter's expedited plan.

When our daughter's fourth birthday rolled around, and she did not receive her baby sister, she was visibly disappointed. We tried to explain that we were working on it, but that it was going to take a while longer.

"How much mo-o-o-o-o-ore?" she whined at us.

"We told you. Santa needs to come two more times, then we will all go to China to get your sister."

We were anticipating a match, not that spring, but the following one. It was hard to see our daughter's disappointment, but there really wasn't too much we could do about it. Or was there?

We'd heard that there were some expedited referrals available through various special needs and designated matching programs, so we asked our agency to investigate on our behalf. After weighing all the pros and cons, we arranged to participate in the special needs program and selected a child.

It was at the very first of November when I found our daughter playing 'Tea for Two' in her room. "Who are you having tea with?"

"My sister," she replied.

I began my usual lecture about more visits from Santa, but she was adamant that her sister was coming very soon. "She's going to be the best Christmas present ever," she informed me. I left the room wishing it were so.

That very afternoon, we found out the China Center of Adoption Affairs had already matched us, and a travel notice had been issued! We could go and complete the adoption just as soon as arrangements could be made.

We spent that Christmas in China with our daughter and her new baby sister. She was right. Mei Mei was the best Christmas present ever.

That would be the perfect end to the story, right? But last week, both of our daughters came to us and informed us they were ready for a baby sister.

FULL CIRCLE

My husband and I had been married for 16 years, and had made all the attempts to be a family with children. They didn't pan out. When we'd tried to adopt an infant in our state years earlier, we were told there was a waiting list of four years, with a maximum age of 40. My husband was 37. The simple math came down to 37+4=41. They told us we had aged out of their system, and they could not help us.

We got over it. Sort of. We had a good life with nieces and nephews and the requisite dog. We could have tried other avenues, but for several reasons, my husband thought we just weren't in a position to continue seeking a private adoption, an international adoption, or adoption in any other way. So, we worked, and traveled, and were relatively content as a couple.

Then, my beloved dad, my hero, passed away. Three days later, we held his memorial service. My sister decided that my three brothers, she, and I should sing an old choir piece at the service. It was the benediction we used to sing at our church.

> *The Lord bless you and keep you.*
> *The Lord lift his countenance upon you*
> *And give you peace.*
> *The Lord make his face to shine upon you*
> *And be gracious, gracious unto you. Amen.*

It was a beautiful choral piece, and with the help of some wonderful church choir friends, we did it for Dad.

When it truly sank in that he was gone, I was devastated. I cried all the time. I was so sad. I think that changed my husband's heart. One day about six weeks after Dad's death, Ron saw an article about a couple our ages adopting a baby from China. In the car on the way to church, he told me he had seen the article and thought we should look into it.

I guess I really wasn't perfectly content as a childless family. The very next morning I was at the doorstep of our local international adoption agency. We got the paperwork and started on the road to adopting a baby from China. This was at the time when "the wait" was measured in months. Ha! We became enmeshed in one of the first of the slowdowns at the China Center of Adoption Affairs.

I waited patiently, for the most part. I didn't call the agency. I didn't bug our social worker. Then on the Friday before Mother's Day, I decided I'd earned a call to the agency. I just wanted to know if they really had our paperwork in China or if it had all been lost. I called, asking if they could give me a status report. The agency contact replied, "I have your referral information in front of me. Are you ready for the news?"

Wow! She gave me my daughter's name, her health status, where she was from, and...her birthday. It didn't sink in until I called to tell my family. Her birthday was the same day we said goodbye to Dad at the church. We didn't have a clue then that we would be adopting a baby. Absolutely no idea. God had worked in mysterious and wonderful ways.

On that Friday before Mother's Day, I became a mother. What an incredible first Mother's Day celebration we had! Our church gave us the alter flowers from the Mother's Day services, and we celebrated with two other families whose referrals also came that same Friday.

It's true that there is a red thread that binds the lives of those meant to be together. Dad had a red thread that bound his Chinese granddaughter to him. It brought us comfort and the beginning of so much joy.

WHAT'S UP, DOC?

We were having such a busy day at my pediatric office, I didn't even have the long-awaited call on my mind. I was inundated with colds, strep throat, and getting school shots done before the beginning of the new school year.

I was with a patient when my receptionist interrupted me. "Dr. Sumner, there's a call from (she listed the acronym for my adoption agency). Do you need to take it?"

In one amazing leap, I was up to the top of the stairs. I'm sure I frightened some of my young patients with as much noise as I made in getting to my office so quickly. I knew exactly who it was and I was afraid I would start crying! I didn't want anyone to see me. How silly, in retrospect!) I did cry with joy all afternoon, as did half my staff and patients.

When told that my daughter's Chinese name meant happy and beautiful, I felt like the proudest mother in the whole world!

The patients who shared in my tears of joy still remind me every time they return that they were in my office that day. They still remember me bursting through the office door, screaming with excitement – and it is just as precious every time we relive it!

To know the road

ahead, ask those

coming back.

Chinese Proverb

BUT IT'S ALREADY DECORATED

It was a simple matter of arithmetic. Working with hundreds, even thousands of people at the adoption agency exposed me to a fabulous mixture of personalities and interests. It was bound to happen that, on occasion, I would naturally click with somebody. It might mean an on-going friendship, or just an association beyond the normal agency-client relationship. Shawna had definitely moved beyond client. Her match was due in the next round.

I was astounded to learn that she had been referred a boy! It looked like it might be better for my boss to make the call, so the information was turned over to her. As it happened, the family wasn't reachable at that time so the call was eventually handed back to me.

"Shawna", I began immediately, once I finally got her on the phone, "do you remember how you marked 'either' on your original application with regard to the gender of your child?"

"What?"

"Shawna, you've been matched with a boy!"

It seemed like forever before there was a response from the other end of the line!

"We have a boy," she asked, "a BOY?"

"Yes, and they must really like him there, because he looks really well fed." I was looking at the picture of her son, and there was no doubt that somebody was taking very good care of him.

"This doesn't work! I just finished decorating the nursery."

"What color is it?" This seemed like an absurd conversation to be having, but I had long ago learned that during a match call you go wherever the parent needs you to go. Did I mention that Shawna is an interior decorator?

"Blue."

"Blue? Shawna, that's perfect! It's a boy!"

"No, there are little bunnies all over the place."

The conversation was becoming surreal. I needed to figure out something quickly, but I was concentrating so hard on not laughing out loud, I could barely think!

"Shawna, he is a rabbit. He was born in the Year of the Rabbit. The room will be perfect." It was time to get on with the important details, like his birthdate, height, weight, and the like. She listened intently while I gave her all the information.

"Are you okay with this?" I was afraid to ask, but we needed to know.

"Uh-huh." She didn't sound too convincing.

"Are you sure?" Another few seconds of utter silence and suddenly, from the other end of the line there came an excited jumble of words.

"I-can't-talk-anymore-right-now-my-daughter-is-a-boy-it's-a-boy-I-have-a-son-I-have-to-call-my-husband-I-HAVE-TO-TELL-MY-HUSBAND-HE-HAS-A-SON!"

The phone went dead, and I came to life. All the laughter I'd been suppressing burst forth along with relief. There was no doubt Shawna was absolutely, deliriously happy. So was I!

like me

I was a special needs child. Back in my day, special needs meant you had something pretty seriously wrong with you, and if you had something pretty seriously wrong with you, people were not always kind.

It had taken a lot, but I was proud of the fact that I had overcome my special needs. I finished college. I married. I had two children. I had a great job. Yet there was always something still missing for me.

When I first learned about China's special needs program, I was immediately interested. What better way to serve a child who was in the same boat I had been in, than to take her into my home and share a wonderful life with her? Unfortunately, my family did not feel the same, at least at first. When I told everyone I thought we should consider a special needs adoption my pre-teen daughter burst into tears. My teenage son stared at me in stony silence. My husband simply asked where the idea had come from.

That Sunday there was an orphan ministry presentation at our church. I didn't say anything, but I led my family through the tables and presentations. It's true that some of the materials were shocking. The pictures of malnourishment tugged at the heart, but some of the pictures of the missing and malformed limbs and the cleft lips were more than difficult to see. I was concerned that maybe I had gone into this with rose-colored glasses, or at least glasses filtered by own personal experiences.

I saw tears in my husband's eyes, but my kids just looked miserable. We made it through the presentations, but drove home in total silence. I stayed quiet because I was afraid of what everyone was thinking.

We sat down to our usual Sunday dinner, but the air was so thick with tension I wasn't sure any of us would be able to eat. My husband began to give thanks for our food, but as he continued he asked for guidance for not only himself but the entire family as we embarked upon our adoption journey.

I lifted my head slowly, not wanting the kids to see my tears and not wanting to see their reactions to the decision their father had reached. I was so grateful for his quiet support, but I was so worried about the kids. No "amens" followed my husband's prayer. There was only a miserable, uncomfortable silence.

Finally, my husband announced that we were going to have a very honest conversation about things we had never discussed before. The next three hours were some of the most enlightening I have ever endured or enjoyed. I heard about fights my children had been in over disparaging remarks made about their mother. I heard my son's fears about having to care for a disabled child long after we were gone. I learned that my daughter had been embarrassed all of her life about my conditions. What I heard loudest was that neither child had ever realized how bad conditions could be for me or for orphans. They were more than ready to have us pursue the adoption.

Within a couple years, we brought home not one, but two, special needs children. But times have changed. Medical advances have been so incredible, no one but our family would ever realize both our girls have the same special need I do. And those reluctant kids of mine? Both plan to someday adopt special needs children.

A Father's Tears

Most of the time, adoption agency employees deal with the mom-to-be as the primary contact, but occasionally it's the father-to-be that consistently communicates with us.

Jim was one of those. Jim had a plan. Jim communicated his plan daily. His calls became so frequent that it was no longer necessary to announce his full name. The receptionist buzzed me, often several times a day with, "Jim is on line three for you." Only one other person was announced to me that way, and I was married to him.

An engineer by trade, Jim was a very exacting man. With a military demeanor and the precision to match, he kept me informed of flight numbers, departure plans, and arrival times. He detailed for me exactly where he needed to be in any particular airport in order for his myriad of electronic communication devices to work. He actually told me precisely how long it should take to get to each "optimum communication location." I could then reach him on his cell phone, his back-up cell phone… you get the idea.

On the day Jim's child referral arrived, I diligently dialed every one of his mobile numbers, leaving message after message. When he hadn't returned the calls within a few minutes, I phoned his secretary and demanded to know just what was going on. I just couldn't believe, after all the calls, all the schedule tracking, all the minutia of information I had faithfully recorded, I couldn't find this man on one of the most important days of his life!

Jim's secretary told me he was "local" that day, which was why I couldn't reach him. While in his hometown he didn't carry all of the extraneous equipment. She said she would beep him on his local pager – the one number I did not have. She was sure he would call me back immediately.

After 10 minutes, Jim hadn't called and there were a number of other families waiting for their own glorious news. I dialed an anxiously await-ing mom and was sharing the details about her bundle of joy when our receptionist began frantically waving a note in front of me.

It read:

Jim, on line 6.

Trying to split my concentration between the phone call and the note, I hastily wrote:

Ask 4 # – will call him back!!!

The receptionist returned with a new note:

Will NOT hang up. Will hold!!!

That was "my" Jim, all right. Still, I was determined not to hurry the phone call that I was on. After all, it was a match call, too! I figured Jim would end up leaving a number and I would get back to him as quickly as possible.

Some 15 minutes later, I stared in amazement at the little red blink-ing light representing line 6. He really had hung on all that time. I hur-riedly pressed the button, and inquired, "Jim?"

From the other end of the line, nearly incomprehensible amongst the intensity of his emotions came, "JUST (gulp) TELL ME (sob) I (sob)

AM (gasp) A (sob) (sob) DADDY!"

I don't remember how I got the point across that he was, indeed, a father. I know I immediately joined him in the sobfest. We cried together a long while that day, before I gently reminded him that he still needed to get the news to his wife.

Better to light a candle

than to curse the

darkness.

Chinese Proverb

Well-Prepared... Kinda

I was in my upstairs home office on a business call with my manager, so when the home phone rang my husband, Ben, answered it. He then stood at the bottom of the stairs and yelled up to me to get on the phone. Well, this just drives me crazy, so I ignored him.

"You really need to take this call!" he yelled again, this time with more urgency.

Again, I attempted to ignore him. Not giving up, he yelled one more time. After asking my manager to please hold for a moment, I explained to my husband in a very annoyed voice that I was on the phone and wasn't it obvious that I was ignoring his yelling? Finally Ben burst out with, "It is THE call!"

I have no clue what I said to my manager, but I do still report to her so it must not have been too unprofessional! I was off the phone in seconds. I grabbed the other house phone from upstairs and ran down so that we could both be in the same room to hear the news. There, sitting at my grandmother's old farm table, we learned the news about our daughter.

She was described as a sweet girl, healthy, who liked to smile a lot. She was at a social welfare institute in the province of Hunan. She was born on October 21st...

"What? October 21st?" My smile faded and my stomach dropped. I must have cried out because the woman on the phone paused and then asked, "Are you okay?"

"No," I wailed, "You must have called the wrong people! This baby is only seven-and-a-half months old! She cannot be ours, we are older parents. We were told to expect a child between 18 and 24 months old."

Although we had wanted a younger child, we had been warned that based on our combined ages, we were really eligible for an older child; and would most likely not receive a child younger than 18 months. This had taken some getting used to, but after some time, we'd gotten excited about getting a toddler.

Imagine my surprise when the representative said, "No, I did not make a mistake. You have been blessed with a younger child. Even though you needed to be prepared to accept an older child, that does not mean that you could not have been assigned a younger child."

Well... we were prepared for an older child. Let me tell you just how prepared! I had spent 12 months shopping for everything that a 18-24 month old child could possibly need. I was the garage sale queen. I found resale shops that other people had never heard of!

I had *nothing* for a baby. I knew *nothing* about a baby. And I knew better than to think that my husband or older stepsons were going to be any help in this area. All my careful planning and organization needed to be revisited in a hurry!

One of the first things that we did was to borrow a crib. It was quite a sight to see my 49-year-old husband and my 23-year-old stepson working together to put the crib together for our newest family member. I still remember Ben's exclamations as they worked.

"The last time I did this, it was for *you*!" said my husband to his eldest child, "I can't believe I'm doing it again for *me*!"

Return Phone Calls

It was a Wednesday, our usual day for the Department Manager meeting. I'd been following the Adopt-Parents-China Internet list closely and I knew my referral was going to be coming soon. I'd even been telling my friends and coworkers about it for a couple of weeks.

Our meeting was held in the largest office in the department, which is where the secretary's desk was located. Her telephone quietly rang whenever any of the phones in the department rang. She could tell who was receiving the call. We could also tell if the call was coming from inside or outside the hospital. An internal call was a single ring, while an outside call was a double ring. During the meeting, if I heard a double ring, I'd look over at her and she'd either shake her head "yes" or "no."

On one double ring I looked over and she shook her head "yes." I turned my back to the meeting and used the phone at the desk where I was sitting to pick up my call.

"Hello, this is Gigi," I said into the receiver.

"Gigi, this is Sandra, from the agency." My heart began to flutter. She said, "I'm returning your call from yesterday."

My heart sank. I'd called my agency the day before with some bogus question and had left it on her voicemail.

Sandra continued, "And to let you know you are a mommy!"

My heart really started pounding. I began to cry with joy. She asked me not to cry, saying she'd start crying, too.

"I'm not crying," I lied, as Sandra promptly started crying with me.

She filled me in on my daughter's info – birth weight, birth date, orphanage, location – everything she had on my new daughter. By then, I was crying, smiling and trembling all at the same time. Somehow, I managed to get everything written down.

Finally, the call was over. I turned around, grinning ear-to-ear, and told my boss, "Yes, that was 'the call'…I'm a mommy!" He stopped the meeting and said a prayer for my daughter and me. He then tried to restart the meeting. Fat chance! I had calls to make!

I excused myself and went through the kitchen back to my office, sharing my good news with everyone I saw. I had to share – it was obvious I'd been crying, but I was grinning ear to ear. I was smiling so big and so much, it made my cheeks hurt!

A Fairy Tale Ending

When I was a young girl, I was a complete romantic. I truly believed that one day a handsome prince would ride in on a stalwart steed and whisk me away to a castle. As I got a little older, some of my naivety went away, but secretly, I still believed in fairy tales. I thought the fairy tale had come true when I met and married the most wonderful man on the planet. He understood my need for that magic and even agreed to a Disney wedding!

We set out on the wonderful adventure that was to become our lives, traveling extensively for a few years before finally settling into our "castle." I enjoyed every minute of the painting, decorating, and creating. Before long we had a wonderful place. We were ready to begin the next phase – nesting.

Life had been a fairytale, but it seemed to all come crashing down when we learned there would be no children for us. We didn't have to do a lot of testing or endure procedures. Our situation was instantaneously recognizable to the specialists. It was also final. There would be no little prince or princess in the castle.

We had never discussed adoption, but one Sunday representatives from an international adoption agency came and spoke before a large group of us. I was mostly there because I was assigned refreshment duty, but I did listen to what was being presented.

Obviously something sunk in because before long, I had convinced my husband that this was an answer for us.

It would be years before dreams came true, but when our first Match Day came, my husband made sure it was magical. Unbeknownst to me, my husband had talked to the agency and let them know that even though I was expecting to receive "the call" it was actually to go to him. He had a very special surprise planned for me.

He had ordered a king's costume, along with a royal purple pillow, and after printing out the match information that he received from the agency, he prepared to present his greatest gift to me.

"You might want to look outside," my co-worker said.

"What? Why?" I replied, but even as I answered him, I was getting up from my seat and heading for the window.

There, in full royal regalia, was my husband on a white horse. While not a knight in shining armor, it was close enough. He beckoned me to come down, pointing at a golden envelope on the overstuffed pillow that he carried. It didn't take me 30 seconds to get down the stairs. In that envelope was the match information on our daughter.

At long last, the fairy tale seemed to be ending as it should. Except it was just the beginning. My husband actually got dressed up like that and rode on his trusty white steed five more times. And the king and queen are living happily ever after with their six little princesses.

Refusing Reality

Match calls are so different now than in the early days. At the agency, the staff had heard every kind of reaction from new parents along the way, but as the years rolled on, the reactions became more and more subdued. It was as if everyone was afraid to believe the dream could come true at last. In one case at our agency, that turned out to be a colossal understatement.

Because we as adoption agency representatives don't know what adoptive parents have shared, or who they've shared with, when we have to leave a message regarding a match, we always try to be as innocuous as possible. The most we say in a first message is something along the lines of "Hi, this is Maggie from the agency. Please return my call as soon as possible. We have some wonderful news for you."

That was pretty much the message I left for Lisa, but when she had not returned my call within a couple hours, I left a second message meant to sound a little more urgent.

"Hi, it's Maggie, again. It's really important that I speak with you today. Please call me back at 555-123-4567 as soon as possible. I am so thrilled with the news I have to share with you!"

Still, there was no return phone call after several hours. I tried Lisa's husband, but was told he was out of town for the remainder of the week. For the third call to Lisa, I phoned the main switchboard at Lisa's office and asked if she was at work that day. I was assured she was in but had a full schedule, so I left a message with the receptionist.

Nothing. Nada. Zip. Zilch. And now it was the end of our business day. I left one more message in her voicemail letting her know that I was "taking important information for her" with me to my home. I left both my home and cell phone numbers and encouraged her to call, no matter what time it was.

I was busy closing the office for the day, turning out lights, turning off the copier. I was about to leave and lock the door when the phone rang. I ran to pick up, and it was Lisa, at last! She sounded irritated as she asked me what on earth was so urgent. When I told her it was her match call, there was dead silence for a few moments, and then she actually yelled into the phone.

"What a cruel thing to do! How could you make this kind of mistake? You should be fired for this!" she shrieked. I was stunned, but assured her it was not a mistake, and I really was looking at a picture of her daughter.

"You are not!" she yelled. "I am not due for a match for another year! I want to talk to your boss right now! This is unforgivable!"

By now she was crying, and I was pretty darn close to it myself. I could not understand how she didn't know that her match was coming. I could not figure out how to assure her there was no mistake.

"Lisa," I started, "I'm not sure what the mix-up is, but today is your Match Day, and I am going to send you an email with a picture of your daughter! Please, let's just get your husband on a conference call, so we can sort this out."

It took a while to get the conference call going, but Lisa's husband, who seemed just as stunned as she was, said that he would accept the email. In the meantime, I had received permission to email all of the documentation, not just the tiny picture. This was the only way we could assure the two of them of the reality prior to the overnight package that contained the CCCWA's letter of acceptance for them to sign.

It turned out that Lisa had originally been an active participant in a number of online adoption forums, some of whom put forth match predictions. Whether one of those led her astray, or Lisa miscalculated, we will never know, but she had accidentally added a year to her match timing.

Every year I receive a picture postcard of Lisa's daughter. Every year, I tear up when I read the note. This year, she sent: "Another year I didn't think I would have. Thank you."

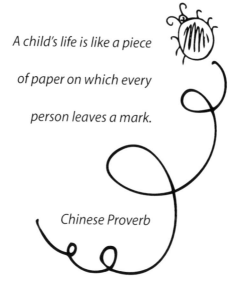

A child's life is like a piece

of paper on which every

person leaves a mark.

Chinese Proverb

MY B-A-B-Y

My second adoption from China was for my baby. My first adopted child was three-and-a-half years old at placement. While I had a very independent, competent, helpful child, I still wanted a baby – *my* baby. I just needed that baby in my arms – physically, mentally, spiritually, and emotionally.

Close to Christmas, there was word that referrals were coming. Late one evening three days before Christmas, my four-year-old daughter went to the closet, put on her red coat, and picked up her backpack. She did this often. As usual, I asked her, "Kate, where are you going?"

"I am going to China. I am going to bring home my sister." I, of course, burst into tears and hugged her.

I have a great respect for the Chinese culture. When I was in China adopting my older daughter, I went into the Shrine of Quan Yin of 1,000 Eyes. I thanked the goddess for my older daughter, and I asked her for another daughter – a baby. MY baby. I know that my request was heard. I got "the call" exactly nine months after my dossier arrived in China.

Again, tears. In my attempts to become a mom, I had tried to adopt domestically for several years; had gone through numerous fertility treatments; and had lost three pregnancies. Now, here was my baby at long last, nearly the same wait as a full-term pregnancy.

"The call" came at work while I was downstairs on a break. I was paged over the PA system, which never happens to me. Of course, all my friends and co-workers knew what was going on. I was not expecting the news at that point. I was both totally calm and rather numb.

A girl, they told me, with a name that meant "super charming" and "fragrant garden." She had a heart murmur and was 14 months old. I still have the notes I scrawled on a little piece of scratch paper. The fact that she had a heart murmur did not even give me pause. I also have a heart problem, and this was not a concern. However, I had asked for a child under eight months, very specifically, for my own reasons. This little girl was 14 months old. Again, I cried.

What was I going to do? She was so much older than I had requested. Would she be the baby I needed? Wanted? Desired? Craved? I went online and found so much support from so many other women who had found themselves in the same situation. They were so honest, so open, and so very helpful. She was small. She was probably developmentally more like a baby. It would be okay.

Still, I couldn't stop crying. My doctor put me on medication for a few days. It calmed me down. For three days, I thought about it. For three days, I talked to anyone and everyone online.

I went ahead with the adoption of my baby. When she was put into my arms two months later, it was indeed okay. More than okay. She was exactly what I needed in every way. We bonded within the hour, something I had never believed in nor experienced. It was absolutely wonderful to have my B-A-B-Y!

MiRacLeS

Sometimes when you are just sitting in the pew expecting to hear some general inspiration, things change abruptly, and you feel like the pastor's words beam directly from his mouth to your heart. That happened to me on the Sunday our church celebrated our ministry for orphans.

For some time, it had been on my mind and in my heart that I wanted to adopt. This particular Sunday, I felt something more. It was as if I was being called to the subject. I didn't know when or how, but that day, I knew I would be adopting. I only hoped my husband agreed.

Imagine my surprise when, at lunch after the service, my husband asked if I would ever consider adoption. As far as we knew, we were able to have biological children, so the subject of adoption had never come up before. My husband confessed to me, and I confessed to him, that there was just something in that morning's sermon that spoke directly to us. To the both of us.

We are not wealthy people. We work hard for our money, so to think about spending a large sum, most of which we didn't have, was daunting. We didn't even know where to begin, so we went back to our ministry and asked questions. Very quickly, we were directed to our agency and two couples that had adopted special needs children from China. These were people that had volunteered to mentor people through the process, and they were so warm and welcoming. I remember being shocked at not worrying about discussing our personal finances with them.

Fortunately, they had ideas for fundraisers, and probably most helpful, they had vast knowledge regarding adoption grants. Before long, we had the money to get started. We hesitated a little because we just weren't sure which special needs we wanted to consider.

I work in special education, so I know very well some of the challenges that these children can have. While I was willing to accept certain special needs, there were others that I was not prepared for.

We talked it over and selected a few minor conditions. We decided we wanted as young a child as possible. We preferred a girl. When we turned in our checklist the agency warned us that it could be a longer wait because our list was "very narrow.," but it was what we felt comfortable with at the time. We were told that we could always broaden the list later.

While we waited for a match, I participated in more and more online forums. As I read each family's experience, I realized that much of what we had eliminated from our list was really very easily managed. It seems like every few weeks I was calling with another condition to add to our list. The agency staff even joked with me that if I would just broaden the age range, I could be matched very quickly.

When we hadn't been sent any child documents to look at after a year, I became a little anxious and began looking at children online. On my third or fourth day of looking, a precious face stared back at me from the computer screen. I felt absolutely compelled, just like on that Sunday the previous year.

We started our adoption asking for a young-as-possible female with minor special needs, and ended up with the perfect addition to our family: a four-year-old boy with a severe but repairable special need. We've never been sure if we chose him, or God chose us for him. Either way, it's the miracle we are grateful for every day.

FLOWER POWER

It was the Friday before Christmas. I was closing up at work for the day to meet my lunch buddies for our annual holiday lunch. By this time, I knew referrals were in and it was just a question of what day. Before Christmas? After Christmas? I knew my agency's number by heart. At least, I thought I did.

Just as I locked up my office desk, the phone rang. I glanced at the screen to see if I should pick it or let voicemail answer. I didn't recognize the number. Intrigued, I went picked up the phone. On the other end was a very gentle and sweet voice.

"Hello, this is the agency," she began, "do you know why I am calling?"

"Yes," I replied, very calmly, "I think so...is this my referral call?"

"Yes," she answered, "I am looking at your beautiful baby!"

I froze for a moment. I thought I was prepared for this call, but everything I'd prepared went right out of my head. I started to rip my purse apart. I was looking for the list of questions that I'd posted by every phone in my house, but... I was at work! Finally, I found a copy of the list in my purse. She began to tell me what my daughter looked like. The one thing that stuck with me was that she said, "She looks very smart!"

Finally, my brain kicked in. I proceeded to grill her with every question I could think of. I was jotting notes all over the place. Hair? Tiny or chubby? In foster care? What did she eat?

Within minutes, my first picture of this absolutely gorgeous baby had arrived in my email. I quickly downloaded the file to my laptop. The phone rang again. It was my lunch buddies wondering where I was.

Well, I thought, *how is it that they could not hear the elation in my voice?* "I'M A MOMMY! I GOT THE CALL!" They ordered me to get to the restaurant and tell them all about it.

We hadn't even been seated, but I gave warning that I was about to become the most obnoxious person they had ever met. I whipped out my laptop to show them the picture and then starting frantically making calls on my cell phone. Thank goodness, I had programmed a list of numbers into the phone! I spent the entire lunch on the phone and staring at my new baby's picture. I have to confess, I'd never enjoyed watching people in restaurants or other public places trying to look "important" with their laptops and cell phones, but – hey, today I was important!

After our joyous celebration of lunch (I'm still not sure if I actually ate anything), I rushed home to continue calling and emailing anyone I could get hold of. By late that afternoon, my one sister and I were online chatting. She had her three girls all standing around anxiously awaiting my email. Finally, it went through. My sister began instant messaging me the girls' reactions one by one. Eventually, my other sister received her picture via email and let me know that my nephews couldn't wait to meet their new cousin.

The very next morning, I was online tracking my referral package. Just as I noticed it had been delivered to my area, the doorbell rang, and I thought, "That's it! That's my package!"

It wasn't. Instead, it was the florist delivering flowers from my brother and sister-in-law. But, as I went to shut the door, I saw a delivery package sandwiched between the two doors. Had it not been for those flowers… who knows when I would have figured it out!

Special Delivery

The rumors were flying. Referrals were supposed to be hitting the United States any day, but nothing was being posted on the Internet lists. I waited until the last possible moment at my office and then headed out for dinner with friends. How I had hoped to announce my baby's arrival at dinner. Now it would be just another long weekend to get through.

The girls tried to get me to accompany them to a dance club after dinner. They begged and cajoled. After all, my "freewheeling ways" would end soon enough once that precious bundle arrived. But, I was a little down in the dumps. I really had thought the referral would be in by now. I was more in the mood for my fuzzy robe and slippers, a classic movie, and maybe some mocha almond fudge ice cream. I excused myself and headed home.

I arrived to find four messages on my voicemail. The agency had been calling me since 15 minutes after I left my office!

"We'll wait here for about another hour," said the first message. Oh, no! that had been several hours earlier!

"We're sorry, but we can't wait any longer. We will go ahead and send your match information via overnight delivery to your home address," said the second message.

So, I had missed the long-awaited call and would only receive written information? I *needed* that human connection!

"We've just learned that, due to your location, the company will not deliver on a next-day basis, so your package won't actually arrive until Monday" said the tired and obviously disappointed voice on the third message. There was no way I was going to make it to Monday!

"You know, we've been discussing your case and we realize just how hard it will be for you to wait through the weekend. We're having one of the agency representatives take a copy of the information home with them. They will try to call you from their home," announced the final message. Great! Uh… when? When would they try to call me?

I looked at the clock. It was nearly midnight in my agency's time zone. I came to the painful realization that I was going to have to make it through at least that night without any information on my match. I sobbed and sobbed as I donned my robe, stood in front of the refrigerator, and began spooning ice cream directly from the carton.

When the phone rang, I was so startled that I dropped both my spoon and the ice cream carton on the kitchen floor as I ran for the living room. "Huh-wo," my words were as strangled from the sobs as from that mouthful of ice cream, "Is dis duh agency?"

"Kind of," said the voice at the other end, "Are you okay?"

"I'm better now," I managed to get out as I swallowed the last of my frozen treat.

Then the angel that had waited up until nearly midnight proceeded to give me all the information about the most beautiful child in the world. We talked for a very, very long time. I just didn't want to let her go! She emailed me the picture. Ten minutes after we hung up, I printed the picture that I would take to bed with me.

The next morning, I was on my hands and knees on the kitchen floor scrubbing up the gooey mess made by the completely forgotten ice cream when the doorbell rang. In addition to those calls to me, my agency had talked long and hard to the delivery company. They found out one of the delivery company's employees actually lived in my town, so they talked him into making a "special delivery" of my "special delivery" on a Saturday!

Happy Holidays

What I remember about "the call" was that I had been sad and depressed. We had been expecting our referral around October, as that was the way the match timing was working out. October came and went. November came and went. As December began, I wasn't really in the mood to celebrate all the wonderful Christmas happenings. I just wanted my baby.

My husband had been in town to celebrate Christmas with me. He was working in Hawaii while I stayed at home to work. We had to celebrate before Christmas, as he didn't have time off at the actual holiday. We had both made the comment that the call would probably come the day he left. He flew out at 9 a.m. Monday morning and I went to work.

I must have checked voicemail 100 times that day. I got so good at calling the agency recording I'm surprised I didn't wear it out! Finally, at 3 p.m., I checked voicemail again, and there it was, the message I'd been dying to hear.

"Congratulations, you have a beautiful daughter!" The message said to call the agency back, and I did, saying I'd be at their office very shortly.

As soon as I hung up, I screamed "SHE'S HERE!" and my coworkers came running over to see what was going on. We were all jumping up and down and crying. They all but pushed me out the door.

It was a quick ride. At the agency, I was handed a picture of a beautiful little girl. I could not stop staring at it. She was only about three months old in the picture, and she was now eight months. Oh, how I wanted to hold her that very second.

Talk about terrible timing! I couldn't reach my husband to tell him the wonderful news, since he was still in the air over the Pacific Ocean. It was not until nearly midnight that I was able to call him and tell him he was a daddy. That was the most wonderful Christmas present we ever received. And since our daughter was placed in our arms on Valentine's Day, that holiday is pretty special in our lives, too!

CROSSING That BRIDGE

We were an older couple, ages 56 and 60. We had asked for the youngest child possible, but were expecting up to a five year old. We had no idea what age our angel would be.

I was driving across a bridge over the James River when the call came. I had a cell phone that I never used, but I'd started carrying it while in process.

When I answered, our social worker told me that we had a daughter, and she was two years old. I couldn't speak! I had to get across the bridge and pull over to the side of the road so she could give me the details. At first I was a little disappointed, since we had hoped for a baby, and this baby was already two. On the other hand, I was elated she was younger than three!

I was so excited I wanted to tell everybody, but my husband and our six other children were at soccer practice. No one was home! After I stopped shaking, I wiped the tears away so I could see. Then I drove to the practice. My husband and a good friend knew something was up when I showed up late and obviously had been crying. We all stood on the soccer field hugging and crying with joy over the news of our daughter.

We became a forever family in June. I wouldn't have wanted any other child but her. She was definitely the right choice for us.

Be not afraid of growing

slowly, be only afraid

of standing still.

Chinese Proverb

control issues

As much as I know I shouldn't try to control everything, I continue to be disappointed when I can't.

I had been carrying around a cell phone like it was a part of me for weeks with a number known only to my husband, my parents, and our adoption agency. I not only dutifully carried that phone everywhere, I actually treated it as something to be worshipped.

One afternoon I'd been away from home, cell phone in hand, of course. I returned home to find a strange van in my driveway. I couldn't imagine who it could be. But when the garage door opened, my husband was standing there, and I realized he must have come home early in one of the company vans.

When I questioned him about what was going on, he explained that he'd needed to get hold of me, but hadn't been able to get through on the cell. I said the phone had been on all day, and immediately went to the phone in the kitchen to call my cell to make sure it was working. As I listened to the mechanical voice saying "all circuits are busy" I was also half listening to my husband saying something about wanting to show me a picture in a motorcycle magazine.

"No, not now, I've got to figure out what's wrong with this phone. I'm really counting on it right now."

I turned back to pick up the kitchen phone, ready to dial again. As I did, my husband placed in front of me two pictures of the sweetest baby

I'd ever seen, coupled with a medical report.

"Don't you want to see your baby?" he asked.

I nearly fell over in disbelief. It turned out both he and the agency had been trying to reach me for more than an hour. Since neither could get through to my cell, he'd finally jumped in the company van and raced over to the agency. The place was so frenzied, he nearly got into an accident in the parking lot, but he made it into the office, picked up the paperwork and raced home.

In the end, I couldn't control how it all shook out. I wanted to be the one to get "the call." I'd been waiting for so long. I learned sometimes being out of control is a good thing, because once I saw her pictures, being in control of "the call" didn't matter at all. All that mattered was the child in that amazing little photograph.

a Really Good Hair Day

On the day that would end up being our Match Day, mid-morning I was surfing the Internet like crazy. I was filled with anticipation, excitement, and nervousness. Truthfully, I felt a little sick to my stomach. Even my husband had suffered a slight case of nausea earlier that day.

There were rumors our group was up next for referrals, but I was tired of waiting and wondering. I had a hair appointment scheduled that afternoon. As I walked out the door, my phone rang. I wondered if that could be "the call," but inexplicably, I locked the door anyway. Yes, I ignored my gut feeling and went ahead to my appointment.

When I arrived home, I couldn't get the door open fast enough. I literally ran to check the voicemail and listened to the one and only message. It said to call my agency immediately as they had great news to give me. They wanted to talk to me personally.

I shook so hard. I couldn't concentrate. I had trouble breathing. I cried during the entire conversation. Our poor agency representative had to keep repeating herself.

She told me that we had a beautiful daughter. She was holding her picture in her hand. I was given the information that my daughter was coming from the southern most tip of China, near Hong Kong. She was nine-and-a-half months old, had been in an orphanage briefly and was now in foster care. Her name meant "little bamboo".

At last, my dream of having a daughter was fulfilled! I called my husband first. He was driving, so he had to pull onto the side of the road in order to take in all of my information. Next, I called my mother and simply told her that she was a grandmother.

"*I am?*" She choked out. She was so happy she could barely breathe!

We were the first family in our agency "world" to announce our referral on the Internet. Then, the news of referrals began to spread like wildfire. I could not keep up with the congratulatory emails we received from all over the world. Many people couldn't wait to hear the details and called me. My phone line was busy the rest of that evening. But, it was when we received the picture from our agency by email that I truly realized that we indeed had a daughter.

OPPOSITES ATTRACT

I was in a particularly stressful period in my life. While working a full-time job and eagerly anticipating the referral of my long-awaited daughter, I pushed myself to finish a graduate degree. I was worried that the referral call would never come and terrified that I wouldn't finish my thesis before the momentous phone conversation that would change the course of my life.

Some of my academic colleagues and graduate student friends silently worried that "I had no idea what I was getting myself into as a single mother." They were, after all, well acquainted with my professional interests and intellectual pursuits.

In my heart I knew that motherhood, and even impending motherhood, would lead to dramatic shifts in my priorities making it difficult, if not impossible, to complete my degree. So I struggled to compartmentalize my inner life. I immersed myself in the rewarding, agonizing, and all-consuming project of writing my thesis. Time passed quickly. I never did decorate the nursery or sew the baby clothes.

One afternoon in April, I found myself photocopying and compiling the final copies of my thesis. I had beaten the clock. I was exhausted but relieved. I sent a playful email message to my thesis advisor proclaiming "I AM FREE!"

I had filed my taxes two days earlier. My graduate work was behind me. I was ready for a vacation… or just a good night's sleep. It was time to exhale and clear my mind for life's next adventure.

It was the quickest exhale in history! The start of that adventure, the all-important referral call, came less than two hours later.

I was, of course, thrilled to hear the glowing report of my daughter's beauty and good health. The agency representative gushed that this was an unusually adorable and petite child. I hadn't given much thought one way or the other about the height of the child I would be referred. But for some reason, at that particular moment, I began to think about family get-togethers at my parents' home. Everyone in my immediate family is tall. I imagined all of us towering over my child. In my dazed and fatigued state, I tried but could not fathom a petite Chinese girl in our midst. From nowhere I blurted out, "I am six feet tall!"

In her infinite wisdom, the representative simply replied that my new daughter and I would be very cute together. And, in truth, my daughter fits beautifully into our extended family. She is as petite as I am tall, but her personality and zest for life are large enough to fill my heart and the hearts of all who love her.

This was the perfect child for me, regardless of her height. She has brought so much joy to our lives that we all feel ten feet tall.

AnniveRSaRy ExtRaORdinaIRE

We were anticipating our referral in late spring or early summer. That was an especially busy and magical time for our homegrown daughter and for us. For her, there was a prom, an awards ceremony, and a speech at 8th grade graduation that reminded me of just how grown up and aware of the world she had become.

For me, there was my employment as a youth counselor, trying to maintain a reasonable home environment, and making time for dates with my husband, who was working as a computer software engineer. With everything that was going on, I was kept too busy to suffer from the all too common anxiety over when we would get "the call."

With the end of May came the end of many of my daughter's activities. They'd kept my mind occupied. Now, I paid more attention to the adoption rumors. We learned the group ahead of us, which included a local family, had still not received their referrals. That made us, especially me, more anxious. We found out that one group ahead of us had their referrals lost in the mail for a time, which did nothing for my nerves, of course.

June arrived – our anniversary month. Knowing it might be our last chance for a getaway since we were expecting a two-year old, we decided to plan a special anniversary trip to St. Augustine, a favorite for both of us. This was to be our fourth anniversary, traditionally marked by linens.

A bed and breakfast seemed especially appropriate; the bed linens could be counted on to be a charming print, and the breakfast table would be set with linen napkins. We made the arrangements to stay at the bed and breakfast where we'd stayed before. We readied ourselves for the trip to the land of Spanish architecture, horse drawn carriages, and Victorian claw foot bathtubs. It would be very special.

The day before our anniversary, as we were packing to leave, I commented to my husband that we should let the agency know where we would be, just in case. As the time for referral neared, it was important for them to be able to reach us wherever we were.

I was carrying the phone into the bedroom and began punching in the number. I told the receptionist who I was and why I was calling. She asked me to please hold for a moment.

The next thing I knew, an agency representative was on the line asking me if I was sitting down. I sat down on the edge on the bed. (There's that linen connection again!) She continued, "I'm looking at a picture of your daughter and she's beautiful!" I let out a squeal and turned excitedly to my husband to tell him the news. Seeing my reaction, he'd figured it out on his own.

We told her our plans, and arrangements were made to overnight the pictures directly to the bed and breakfast. Needless to say, we didn't get away quite as soon as we'd planned. After all, I had to call the entire immediate world and let everyone in on our news!

When we did finally pull out of our driveway, we didn't drive, we floated to our destination! I kept marveling at what an awesome anniversary present we were about to receive. Upon our arrival, we excitedly let the owners of the bed and breakfast know what was happening and that we would be looking for that overnight package.

What an anniversary present! Nothing could ever top that. That day will forever be a double reason for celebration for us!

Meager to Magnificent

Thanks to my online LID* group friends, I endured the long wait to referral. The "March-ers" with my agency were growing anxious as we each passed the expected referral date mark, but we weren't totally in the dark. Our agency dutifully kept us informed of the progress of our dossiers.

Our cohorts who'd been on the other side of the split were also LIDs in the same month as we were, but their dossiers had moved with an earlier bunch. They shared their experience of the highly conservative nature of our agency's reports with us. This news put us all on edge, as we realized the call could now come at any moment.

A call did come. Well, kind of. My friend in Florida sent an instant message: WE GOT THE CALL! she typed, sharing the happy news of their daughter. My heart raced as I sat in my office. Would they call me next? Was it alphabetical, and their "C" family was contacted ahead of me, an "S?"

I had a lunch date with a close friend. Dare I leave the office, even with cell phone in hand? I was too nervous to eat and was too nervous to wait by the phone in my small workplace. Off I went to meet my friend at the natural foods store.

LID - Log In Date: The day a family's dossier is logged into the Chinese adoption system in China.

As I waited for her by the door, I grabbed a flyer about some yoga class, just in case I'd need paper handy. She arrived and we assembled salads – mine most meager – and grabbed a booth at the front of the store.

I picked at chickpeas. I slid salmon around the plate. And then my cell phone rang. I fumbled in my purse for it and pulled the green yoga flyer closer.

"Hello?" I said in a quivering voice.

"This is the agency. You have a daughter!"

My hand shook so much as I tried to write that my friend came around to my side of the booth to hold the paper. When I look at the page today I don't recognize my handwriting at all. The words are randomly scattered about and the penmanship, well…

I raced back to work, where her picture was arriving by email. My coworkers were back from lunch, too, and when I told them of the referral call, one was kind enough to photograph me opening it. I made them hover at a distance as I pressed the enter key. I was wary of the broad range of referral photos I'd seen, and I wanted that special once in a lifetime moment all to myself.

"Oh, she's beautiful!" I thought, or maybe said, as the tears came.

I grabbed a tissue, then let them at us with the camera.

And That Was That

We stayed in touch with a lot of families during our long wait. During that time, we saw many others come home with children through the special needs program, but this was going to be our first child. We wanted to try the healthy child route first.

As the years came and went, we grew more and more discouraged. Every time the agency contacted us, there was never any news. Doing any kind of update for our home study seemed absurd, since nobody could tell us when, or even if, we would ever get a match. It got to the point where we stopped being involved with the online groups. We stopped checking in with the agency. We basically put the adoption on a back burner and tried to get on with our lives.

When the call finally came, we realized that we had been living in a state of suspended belief for years! We expected to feel excitement. We expected to be overjoyed. What we felt was a little bit of relief and maybe some disappointment that the child we were matched with was much older than we originally requested. I can't believe it now, but for a brief few days, we considered not accepting the match.

It had just been too long. Too much life had happened in the years we had waited. It almost seemed like there would be too little time left with a child. And when we learned of the amount of additional paperwork to be completed, we were not happy! Going through yet another home study just seemed ridiculous. Paying more government fees seemed outrageous. Of course, nothing compared to the irritation of having to be fingerprinted for about what felt like the thousandth time. No, it was all going to be too much, and we were not at all sure we wanted to continue.

And then the overnight package came. In it was the match picture we received via email, and there were other pictures as well. Here she was, sitting in a garden looking incredibly forlorn. My husband said with some emotion, "It is so obvious she's posed there, and seems none too happy about it. Her little eyes look so sad."

There she was sitting on a playground piece looking frightened. "My goodness!" I exclaimed with a tinge of anger in my voice, "How could they have put such a little girl on that by herself?" My previously untapped Mommy Instinct irrationally kicked in, and I felt instantly protective of the little face staring back at me. "Didn't they realize she could get hurt? Didn't they see the look of fear on her face?"

My husband was practically shouting now, "Didn't they realize this was a little girl, our little girl, and we would wonder about those facial expressions? Didn't anyone understand that her parents would worry themselves silly?"

We stared at each other, laughing through the tears. She was ours. We knew it. Two photographs had instantaneously turned us into Mama Bear and Papa Bear. It was unexpected, but our eyes and hearts had made the decision. And that was that!

yes

We are the parents of a lot of children. Some are biological. Some are adopted. We often give testimony at adoption ministries, but we never let on who is adopted and who is not when talking about our kids. In the online community people will sometimes ask, because with this many kids there is always some kind of trauma and drama that we're dealing with. I suppose people want to know if the issues are adoption-related. I think most of what we deal with is related more to hormones (several teens and tweens in the house) and logistics. Do you know what it's like to try to get six kids out the door on time for school?

We thought we were done at six. Then about two years ago, through a wonderful and mysterious chain of events, we learned of a little girl in need of a home. Part of her special needs resulted in an inability to grow and thrive. She was very, very fragile and she was barely a toddler. What were we thinking, you might ask? We were thinking yes.

Yes. We questioned our sanity when we realized that we would be giving up the little bit of freedom that comes with all the kids being in school. Yes. We were concerned that this would delay my wife going back to work for at least two or three more years. Yes. We knew with our finances, we were going to have to not only be creative in coming up with adoption funds, but also figure out how to handle the medical costs after she came home. Yes. We dreaded the paperwork process. Yes. We were petrified that one of the kids would be completely inappropriate during the umpteen social worker visits. Yes. We laughed at the crazy ploys we each tried in trying to get the other to refuse, so that it didn't have to be "me" that said no. Yes. We decided as a family to adopt this precious child. And yes, she became one of the greatest blessings we ever received.

The BIG FOUR-0

It was my 40th birthday. My eight-year-old and I spent the afternoon at our local swimming pool. School had only been out for a week and both of us were just beginning to unwind from the end of the school year (I work in the school system). It was a couple months until our anticipated referral date, when my daughter and I walked in, dripping wet, to the sound of the phone ringing.

Hours earlier, my husband has received "the call" at work. Now, you have to keep in mind that although his heart was completely and thoroughly devoted to this adoption, he was pretty much removed from the paper chase process. He probably couldn't even tell you when our dossier went to China, or even what agency we were using. But at 2 p.m. that afternoon he received a call from a woman who simply said, "I'm looking at a picture of your daughter!" His first reaction was to assume this person was a kidnapper who had somehow grabbed our eight-year-old and wanted a ransom! (We are not wealthy people, but he had quite an imagination.)

"What?!?!?"

"I'm looking at a picture of your daughter." The caller was from our agency, and she repeated herself.

"Who are you?" Bill finally had the presence of mind to ask.

At that point, the agency representative realized she was talking to someone unfamiliar with the language of child referral. She then explained she was calling from the adoption agency and she was holding a picture of our new daughter, who was waiting for us in China. My husband, much relieved, then took down the rest of the information and spent the remainder of the day trying to contact me.

"Does the name Xia Xia mean anything to you?" He asked, when I answered the phone. I didn't know what he was talking about, since I was not anticipating a referral for a few more months. I actually thought he was naming a new restaurant where he was going to take me for my birthday! After I told him no, he filled me in on the rest of the story.

We ended our call with him leaving me with strict orders not to bring our new daughter's picture up on the computer until he got home. Upon his arrival, we all stood around the screen as her beautiful picture appeared. She was, of course, adorable. She was all bundled up in layers upon layers of blankets. There was just a little round face peeking out. We were instantly in love.

And it was the very best way to turn 40.

out of order

Our referral call was a little out of order, as are most things my wife and I are involved with. We thought we were almost at the end of our wait. Needless to say we were both at the end of our rope. Every time the phone rang our hearts would race. After answering, and it not being "the call" the person on the other end could tell... well, that we just didn't want to talk to them.

One afternoon, while my wife was at work, she was paged over the loudspeaker. Our agency was on the phone. Everyone in her office knew that we were waiting for "the call." She started crying. With great anticipation and a sobbing, quivering voice, she answered the phone.

To her (and later my) utter disgust, the agency office manager was just calling to make sure they had our current contact information, because referrals were expected within the week. If my wife could have reached through the phone lines, I believe she would have ripped that poor woman's lungs out!

A few days later I got home from work and was feeling really down. I stopped in the yard and was playing with our two dogs, when I looked up and saw an overnight delivery sticking through the gate of our fence. I nearly fell to my knees!

I grabbed it, ran into the house, and called my wife to see if we had gotten "the call." She was excited, but told me that, no, we had not. We discussed what to do about the delivery. First she told me to look inside, then she told me to wait. Then it was, "Open it, but don't look real hard." I took a quick peek and saw what looked like a passport picture!

My wife raced home from her office, so we could be "introduced" to our daughter together. After crying and screaming with joy, we were off to our local Chinese restaurant to have her papers translated. They were more than happy to do it for us.

When we returned home, we discovered that we had a message in voicemail. Guess who? The office manager had called the previous day to let us know that the shipping company would deliver our referral the next day! We never got "the call." We barely got the voicemail. None of that mattered. We have our daughter.

GROCERY STORE BARGAIN

It was my turn to buy groceries. I hated to buy groceries, so whenever it was my turn, it went like this: I should have gone Sunday afternoon after church, but didn't. I could have gone Monday evening after work, but didn't. Now we were down to a couple steaks in the freezer and some unidentifiable items in the refrigerator vegetable bin. There was no choice. I was going to have to stop on the way home on what had to be the hottest, muggiest, most miserable Tuesday I had ever experienced.

When I called my husband to let him know that I was finally facing up to my responsibilities, he teased me unmercifully. "Babies won't wait, you know," he snickered, "and when they need diapers or formula, they need them now!"

"I know," I replied, with a definite edge in my voice. By that afternoon it was all I could do to drag myself from the office to the car and from the car into the grocery store. At least, when I made it through the doors with my cart, the air was cool and inviting. I wondered if the store management was using air conditioning as a marketing strategy. I was certainly going to remain as long as I could. So began my lazy, noncommittal stroll through the market.

I pushed the cart along, stopping every now and then to take a look at the ingredients on a can or a box. It was rare for me to shop without a list, but that day, I just didn't care. It seemed like it took me a half hour to get down the first aisle, and another 30 minutes to get down the next.

Six aisles later, I came upon the one with the infant goods. Normally, I avoided this aisle, because it reminded me of just how depressingly long the wait had been. I was secretly beginning to despair that our match would never arrive. On this trip, however, my husband's warning that babies didn't wait for mom to be "in the mood" to grocery shop was ringing in my ears. I decided to investigate the disposable diapers and the formula. I was amazed at the array of choices, but finally selected a couple boxes of disposables and a couple cans of formula.

Continuing on through the next few aisles, I was just about to wrap up my shopping when I was shocked to hear my name over the intercom. I was being asked to return to the infant goods aisle. Quickly I checked for my purse, thinking that maybe I had left it or my checkbook, but everything seemed fine.

When I returned to the baby aisle, my husband was standing in the middle with a bouquet of roses, two boxes of diapers, and a picture of the sweetest little face I had ever seen! He swept me into his arms and said he would like to introduce me to our daughter. Naturally, I burst into tears. Behind me, there came a burst of applause. I hadn't realized it, but most of the staff and several customers had been in on the secret!

It was hard to actually finish the grocery shopping that day, but I haven't had any trouble getting my shopping done since then. Unless you count the fact that I continually have to put back the extra things my daughter grabs when I'm not watching her carefully enough!

The Cart Before the Horse

During the adoption process, I had become so enamored of obtaining information about possible dates for referrals that I was spending lots of time online. Based upon the available updates, I had even created my own spreadsheet for possible referral dates.

When other families whose dossiers had arrived in China at the same time as mine started to receive their referrals, I got really nervous and called my social worker. She didn't have any information. The agency did finally update us a few days later. Matches would arrive later that week or early the next week. Yes! I knew they would be calling soon.

In the meantime, I'd been corresponding with families in several states. The rumor mill was really active, so I began working from home the following week. I didn't want to miss "the call." Suddenly, on Tuesday, I began to get a flurry of emails from my friends in other states saying, "The packages are coming!" They seemed to roll across my home state in a wave. I kept thinking, "What about the call? I have questions for the call! I have no idea what to do if the order is reversed!"

At the stroke of 10 a.m., I heard the rumbling of the delivery truck coming down my street. I had enough presence of mind to grab my camera, but promptly forgot how to power it on! As the truck was rolling to a stop, I told the driver, "I've been waiting for this delivery for years!"

He looked more than a little worried when I informed him he was the stork and asked if I could take his picture. In the end, he was a good sport, posing with the envelope through multiple retakes and lots of mistakes with the camera, while my hands shook and I kept trying, desperately, not to cry.

Inside the house, I seemingly forgot how to open an envelope and ripped it apart! Out popped a folder with my last name on the cover and inside… the most gorgeous child I have ever seen. I looked at the three photos and fell instantly in love.

The rest was a little more difficult. I kept flipping through the pages, muttering to myself. *It was translated, I know they said it was translated! Why can't I read any of it?*

It took me 10 minutes to find my daughter's birth date, and even longer to determine which orphanage and province. After plowing through what I could, I made a call to the agency, so they could make "the call" back to me! Even though it was a case of the cart before the horse, I still feel like I got "the call" because the agency representative spent a long time on the phone with me. She explained in detail all of the documentation that had come in the package. Without her, I would have just had a cart full of indecipherable paperwork, not an introduction to my daughter.

MORNING DEW

I know that today will be the day. I spend the morning putting a fourth coat of polyurethane on the office floor. I'm trying to keep busy, so I don't obsess over this agonizingly long wait to find out who my daughter is.

I'm supposed to be finishing up painting the generator shed and back porch. Instead, I sit, thinking about how I'm on the brink of having *four* children. I need to get started, but I'm frozen with anticipation!

The first posting from our agency has come through, and it is by a "Clark" family. I try to calculate when the call will come. If they work alphabetically, and if they have 50 calls to make, and they average 10 minutes per call, it could be more than eight hours before I hear anything. Words simply cannot express my anticipation and thanks and gratefulness and… oh, fear and joy… all rolled into one! And it hasn't even happened yet! It's just about 11:45 a.m. and already my stomach hurts.

Finally, at 2:25 p.m. I get… "the call!" Our little girl is a nine-month-old 'earth rabbit'! Naturally, even though I taped the list of referral questions right there on the wall next to the phone, do you think I could remember to ask *anything*? I became a babbling idiot!

"Her name is Lu Lu Lu," she said.

I was in tears, brain totally empty except for "Lu Lu Lu" repeating over and over. *What kind of name is THAT? And what does it mean? What does a Lu Lu Lu look like?* My in-laws would later tell me that Lu

158 / ladybug love

could mean "dew" and that doubled, it could mean "morning dew."
How appropriate for the child of a woman whose favorite Grateful
Dead song is "Morning Dew!"

At first, I'd been almost disappointed to hear she was already nine
months old, and would be eleven months before I held her in my arms.
Then the email arrives with her picture. I see her lovely little face…
WOW! She's pretty. I am so excited, but there is absolutely no one to
tell! The kids are all off shopping and none of my friends are home!
Ack! I have to tell SOMEBODY!

We have to wait for the delivery man to bring additional pictures,
but it isn't a next-day delivery. We're too rural. I keep staring at the
one picture from the email, and I think I see a lot of similarities to my
husband – the shape of her head, her forehead, and eyebrows.

The so-called overnight delivery service finally delivers the long-
awaited extra photographs, and in one, she's in front of a tie-dye back-
ground. Tie-dye? Yet another connection to our old life on the Dead
tour!

I DO THIS ALL the TIME

I answer the phone as usual. "Hi, this is your agency, and this is 'the call'!"

It took a few minutes to get over my initial reaction - which was a pretty loud one! Once I was semi-coherent again, I asked the representative to wait while I conferenced my husband in. I conference people in all that time, but at that moment, it was difficult to remember how to even press a single button. Finally, after three or four tries, I got my husband on the phone, pressed the conference button, and we were all connected at last.

"There's someone on the phone who would like to talk to you, " I informed him.

"Okay," came his hesitant reply from the other end.

"Well..." she began, "This is the agency, and I'm calling about your referral."

"WOW! IT'S HERE!" My hubby's enthusiasm was as loud as mine had been. We listened to the basic information about our daughter and then headed to the agency.

Even though we didn't work far from the agency's location, it was hard to get there that day. Somehow, we managed and were rewarded with a picture of the most beautiful child we had ever seen.

By the end of the day, copies of that picture graced the email boxes of anyone and everyone in our email address book!

Only he that has traveled

the road knows where the

holes are deep.

Chinese Proverb

Ahead of the Curve

The entire adoption system seemed to change between our first and second adoptions. For our first daughter, we had done a simple dossier (I didn't think it was simple at the time, but I later realized those were the good old days) and we filed just once with immigration. We were then on our way to China within about six weeks of our match. The entire process was less than a year.

We waited several years to apply again. Wow! We were shocked at what had changed. The most incredible thing was that we were encouraged to put in a special needs checklist of conditions that we were open to, even before we officially applied with the agency. We were to apply and then hurry our dossier and immigration along once we had accepted a particular child. It seemed so different from the first time, but we knew lots of families who had gone through the new process and everyone said that was the way it worked now. Rumor had it that even in the special needs program it was not unusual to now wait a couple years. This was discouraging, but it was the reality of today, not yesterday.

We were just about done with our dossier. In fact, we were waiting for one last document to come back from the Chinese consulate. We were getting so close, and I was getting so excited! The week before we planned to turn in the dossier, the phone rang. It was one of the very dedicated staff members from our agency. She wanted to know if we would be willing to review a file. "What kind of file?" I asked, not even dreaming that she was referring to a file that might lead to a child match. "Why, a file on a special needs child!" came the shocked reply.

It just didn't occur to me that we might be offered a file before our dossier was in China. But we were. We accepted that file, and that child, wholeheartedly. It took some hard, intense work to get our paperwork finished as quickly as possible. Waiting for travel for months instead of weeks was pretty unbearable, but eventually we travelled to China. Then, we were home with our little blessing. We have spent the last couple years chasing after this very active, curious little wonder. She continues to be ahead of the curve – and us – most of the time.

Hurricane Hannah

The wind was really starting to howl outside. That's usually the first sign the storm is going to arrive sooner rather than later. A lot of people who haven't gone through a hurricane assume it's all about the torrential rain. That's a part of it, but long before the rain arrives, lots of stuff gets tossed around by the wind.

I had gone outside to make sure the bikes and lawn chairs had been put into the shed. I even remembered to use the tiedowns to secure things to the ground. We had lost the shed twice before. I had to close the exterior shutters on the windows. We've lived in hurricane country all our lives, so I was busy, but not worried. After making sure everything was properly stowed, I headed for my car, still sitting out in the driveway. Pulling into the garage, I thought I heard the house phone ring, so I quickly ran in the back door. I wasn't expecting our match for a few more weeks, but you never know!

The line was full of static. I could make out a voice on the other end of the line, but there was no way to tell what was being said. I hung up, wondering if it had been my husband checking on me. I decided I'd better call him, but when I picked up the phone the static was just as bad, if not worse.

The weather outside was really getting ferocious, so I concentrated on finishing our hurricane preparations. With the outside shutters already closed, the house was dark. Really dark. I grabbed the camping flashlights, put one in each room and the remainder in the den – our designated "safe room."

The phone rang again. "Hello, the... from... agency!" I could barely understand, but I knew I'd heard the word "agency."

"I CAN BARELY HEAR YOU!" I screamed into the phone.

"We... daughter!"

There it was! This was "the call" and I wasn't able to hear what they were saying! I started crying, partly out of joy and partly out of frustration. What were they talking about now? I thought I heard them say something about a cell phone, but I wasn't sure.

"Oh, no," I cried, "I really can't hear you. *Please do something!*"

"Cell ph—" came the almost-two-word reply. Then the phone went dead and the lights went out. What did I care if they were calling me from a cell phone? I couldn't hear the phone call that was going to change my life! I fumbled in the darkness. Through my tears, it was impossible to find the flashlights that I had just put in place minutes earlier. When I finally located a flashlight and turned it on, a circle of light hit the back door, now vibrating with the force of the storm. Then, it dawned on me... I had a cell phone in the car! The agency had been telling me to try my own cell phone!

By this time, the rain was hitting hard and was already seeping in through some unsealed areas of the garage. I ignored the fact that I would likely get wet, but felt I needed a shield in case the garage door blew in or something. I crouched down beside the car as I grabbed the phone and dialed the agency number.

Miraculously, the connections went through as if there wasn't a bit of weather trouble anywhere in the vicinity! The receptionist knew exactly who I was and immediately connected me to my agency contact. Before I knew it, I had all of the information on my daughter. When I complained that I wasn't able to write it down, since I was stuck in my "safe" position beside the car, she told me if I checked my cell phone voicemail later, I would find that she'd left all of the particulars for me.

Because of the storm, my husband wasn't able to make it home that night, so he didn't get the good news until the next day when we listened to that precious voicemail together. On that day, we named our daughter Hannah, and she has been affectionately known as "Hurricane Hannah" ever since.

The journey is the

reward.

Chinese Proverb

The Waiting Game

Unlike so many people, I wasn't following every bump, delay, and crisis in the international adoption scene. I wasn't involved on the Internet forums, wasn't pacing the floor, or even really watching the calendar. It seemed like everybody was playing the waiting game, but I was very busy managing my everyday life working, taking care of our son, Jake, and my husband, Jeff, so I really wasn't paying close attention.

Completely oblivious to the fact that it was my Match Day, I was having an ordinary day at work. I went to lunch as usual – no big deal. When I returned, I was told that somebody from the agency had called. I didn't think too much of it, but decided to go ahead and return the call to the agency. I was absolutely shocked when I heard, "This is the call you've been waiting for!" It truly had not occurred to me that was why they were calling.

I couldn't say a word. After a few moments of stunned silence, the agency representative went ahead and shared the basic information about my daughter. She said everything had already been translated to English, and that I would be receiving the package through an overnight service the next day. In the meantime, I could expect to receive a photo that evening in my email.

Watching for the arrival of that picture on my computer screen seemed to take forever, but it was more than well worth it. Jeff, Jake and I all watched as the picture slowly filled in from top to bottom on the screen, revealing our precious girl. She was everything we had hoped for. Even nine-year-old thrilled-to-finally-be-a-big-brother Jake, exclaimed, "What a cutie!" After we allowed ourselves some time to absorb the reality that she was ours, we made several photo prints. We put one in a card and hand-delivered it that evening to her soon-to-be grandparents, who shared our elation at knowing who our next new family member would be. It was a wonderful way to turn an ordinary day into an extraordinary day!

That's when my waiting game began. It would turn out that I would pay my dues in the waiting game, after all. Long after "the call" came, we would be delayed in traveling to get our girl. Due to the SARS situation, we had to wait for a very long time before meeting our girl at last. Finally, we traveled as part of the first group allowed after the crisis was over. She was more than worth the wait!

NeitheR Rain, NOR Ice, NOR...

It was a Friday afternoon and I had been having a horrible day at work. I'm one of those women who suffered years of infertility and mis- carriages. I was in a pretty emotional state waiting for our referral.

When our dossier went to China, the wait was much shorter. The agency told me the timeline would lengthen, but I believed there was a chance things would speed up. I'd secretly latched onto a certain dead- line in my heart and mind. That had long since passed.

After spending a good bit of the morning locked in my office crying and feeling pretty sorry for myself, at lunchtime I went to my doctor's office. I drove through icy rain for my last Hepatitis B shot preparing for travel, then headed back to my office. I was in no mood to work.

I was talking with a couple of my managers when I heard a page over the intercom for my formal name. Everyone at work calls me by my nickname, but I had a newer employee on the information desk. I heard the page and ran for my office. I was too excited and anxious to shut my door, so as I answered the phone, about five of my employees closed in on my doorway.

When the agency representative introduced herself, I started crying hysterically. More employees moved toward my door. I really wanted that door closed for some privacy, but I couldn't tear myself away from the phone. I took notes on everything I was told and couldn't remember to ask anything else. I gave my email address, but must have given it incorrectly.

When I got off of the phone, I knew I needed to call my husband. Most of the people who worked for me now knew about our baby, but my husband didn't know yet! I finally closed the door and called him. He wasn't at his desk, so I let the switchboard pick up the phone. I told the woman at the switchboard that it was an emergency. She put me on hold to try to find him for me. She ended up connecting me with my husband's boss, who said he would look for him. After a little while, he came back on the phone and said he couldn't find him. I think at this point, I may have been incredibly rude. This was important! Finally, after another 15 minutes or so, I got to share our news with my husband.

We sat on the phone together, waiting for her photo to arrive in my email, but nothing came through. Hubby volunteered to call the agency and have them resend the picture to him. While the agency representative was resending the email and talking with my husband, she actually told him our daughter was so cute, she was saving a copy of the picture for herself!

Again, we sat on the phone together and waited for her picture to arrive – this time in my husband's email. When it did, Daddy also said she was really cute and forwarded the picture to me. I cried all over again when I realized that we weren't just being told she was cute – she really was beautiful!

In less than an hour, I had enlargements of her photo and pages marked from the various travel guides where we would be going. (There are definite pluses to working in a bookstore!) My husband worked over an hour away and wouldn't be able to get home for a while, so in spite of the weather, my manager, friends and I went out to celebrate. It was a horrible, cold, icy day in January, but the news I received that day made it one of the best days ever!

FOLLOW the INStRUCtIONS

During the interminable wait, I'd nearly lost my mind. There was a lot of pain in that time, and not just related to the adoption. I'd lost my mother, worried about my father, and even helped an agency staff member through her own medical scare. Re-reading some of my near daily Internet postings from that time can bring back a lot of the anguish.

I was out of town with my father when our referral came. My mother passed away the year before, so I was very protective of my father and went with him to as many things as possible. This was an annual trip that he and my mother had taken many times, so I felt it especially important for me to go with him this time.

I had shopped a little the day of the referral (we were in Pigeon Forge, Tennessee, after all) but wasn't comfortable until I returned to my hotel room and started calling the many numbers I had for the purpose of checking in. I'd emailed my agency with very exact instructions as to whom to call and at what phone numbers. I contacted my husband, who had heard nothing. Then I started calling other people whose dossiers had arrived in China at around the same time ours did. Indeed, several told me that they had received their referrals that day. Where was ours?

My usual agency contact had assured me that, although we had a 28th of the month dossier-to-China date, which sometimes meant missing the cutoff for a round of matches, we were not going to be cut off. I was starting to have my doubts. I called the agency receptionist one more time. I explained that I was expecting my referral, but had not been contacted.

"I do know that all of the referrals have been contacted," she said, "so you must be in the next batch." My heart sank! It had happened to me again. Things had always gone this way for me. Oh, how I sobbed and sobbed! I cried myself to sleep.

A few hours later the phone rang. It was the agency explaining that they had already talked to my son that morning, but they had just noticed my detailed instructions and had decided that it would be a good idea to call me – personally – at the hotel. I wrote down each detail. Then I called my husband, and finally, our sons, who were at home.

"Oh, yeah," commented my older, laid back son, "the agency called this morning." *Grrrrrrr!*

When I received the picture in the hotel lobby, it made my father smile for the first time, in a long time. He bonded with the picture of a baby who would later become his beloved granddaughter.

I carried those pictures with me that night as we went out that night. Of course, the pain of the wait was all worth it! Just ask anybody who has had to put up with my more than frequent blog postings and the emails of "the most darling" pictures of my perfect daughter!

Hua Means Blossom

I knew "the call" would be coming any time, but I didn't know when. During this first adoption process, I didn't have the Internet access I would later have with my second referral. It meant I wasn't able to be so obsessive about the web, and it meant that I had to let my secretary know where I would be.

I was off to a court hearing for an adoption finalization for some of my clients. After the hearing, the family invited me back to their house for a visit, as I wouldn't be able to attend the party they were having later.

Once we arrived at their home, I needed to make use of their facilities. As I headed in that direction, they were asking me when I would get my referral call. I said, "Oh, it could be any time. Maybe sometime during the next few days. We'll see!"

While I was in the restroom, my cell phone rang but I couldn't hear it. The mom came to the bathroom door and told me my phone was ringing, and somehow I just knew this was it. I got really excited and "hurried up" so to speak!

I was right. It was "the call" from the agency! I took the phone into their hallway so I could have some privacy. I remember hearing that our baby was all wrapped up like a little papoose. I remember being told her name, part of which was "Hua." Hua meant blossom, and my last name is a "floral" name. I wondered if that was why the two of us had been matched.

I've never been sure if the agency representative misspoke, or if, in my excitement, I misunderstood, but the birth date I thought I was initially told meant that my baby was 14 months old. Yet when I received the written information, she was a mere nine months of age!

It was about an hour's drive home, and I couldn't stop thinking about my daughter. Cell phone reception on the drive was spotty. I could hardly wait until I could get to a place where I could start calling people.

I'd been struggling with what first name to give her, as I'd already decided to use her Chinese name as her middle name. As I drove, it came to me! Her first name would be Grace, after my Uncle Fuzzy.

Yes, that's unusual. Let me explain. Uncle Fuzzy had died the autumn before I received the news of my daughter. He was my favorite relative – like a second Dad, really. He always said grace before our big family holiday gatherings, and I feel as if he helped God choose my daughter for me. Her name would honor Uncle Fuzzy, and Grace Hua would be two red thread connections for my child.

Hope in the Hospital

After what seemed like endless waiting for our referral, we were starting to think the day was never going to happen. The holidays had passed and we were halfway through January. One night, my phone rang at 11:15 p.m. It was my sister, telling us that my always-healthy Mom was on her way to the hospital, in very serious condition. Ironically, I had just spoken with my Mom an hour before and she was fine. As we rushed to the hospital, my only prayer was for Mom to be okay.

I knew we were next in line for our referral, and this situation seemed so shocking to me. How could this be happening? The thought that my mother might not meet her long-awaited first grandchild? Beyond belief! An hour later we pulled into the hospital and found my mother's condition to be critical. She'd gone into heart failure and was literally saved by my sister, a nurse, performing CPR.

A day later, my mother was transferred to another hospital to undergo more extensive testing. At my office, things were winding down to prepare for a layoff, so I was able to have some time off and be with my mom as she recovered. Her recovery was a miracle in itself.

Every morning that week, I awoke thinking, *Today could be Match Day!* Finally, it was Friday afternoon. On the east coast, it was always nice to know that although it was time for us to go home at 5 p.m., I knew my agency in the western half of the U.S. would be at work for two more hours. That was two more hours to hope for a call!

At quarter of five, I'd just walked across the room to talk to a co-worker when I heard my cell phone ring. As my co-workers told me later, I literally climbed over one of our temporary employees to get to my phone!

When I heard the voice on the other end of the phone say she was calling from the agency, every part of my body went numb. She slowly started telling me about my new daughter. It was totally awe-inspiring to hear details about a real little baby, who, up to this point, had only been in my dreams. After receiving all the details, I called my husband.

My next call was to my mom, still in the hospital. Never in my wildest dreams did I think this call would be made to her there. When Mom heard me call for the second time that day, she knew what it was. She gasped and started to cry so much that the nurses came running to see if she was okay. One of the nurses overheard my mother say "fax" so she popped her head in and said, "Tell her to fax it here!"

That's how our daughter's grandparents saw her for the first time – on a fax print at a hospital. All the nurses were standing around, grinning from ear to ear as they shared in the joyful news. To this day, friends and family say that little faxed picture helped my mom in her recovery.

DReam, DReam, DReam

We were preparing for our first child, a baby girl from China. I'd specifically chosen China because I had always thought I wanted a girl to be my first child. My husband was clueless to this notion, but was so up for a child from China!

Well into a waiting process that had dragged on for an unmercifully long time, one night I had a very unusual, and as it turned out, prophetic, dream. The dream was two-fold. Initially, it was about a couple who were our very good friends. The perfect couple of our social group, they were always happy and seemingly solid. In the dream, I was visiting these friends, and the wife was confiding to me that they were divorcing. This was shocking to me, but even more shocking was that in the dream, the phone rang and it was our agency on the line informing me that we had been referred a boy! Not only was he a boy, but he was older than expected… about 14 months old. Thank goodness my dream ended there!

The very next day, I called "Mrs. Perfect" and told her of my funny dream – at least her part of it. There was dead silence on the other end of the line for a few moments, then she said, "We told *no one* that we are getting a divorce. I can't believe you dreamed about this!" We hadn't seen them in months, so I chalked it up to coinicidence. There was no reason to even consider the other part of the dream. A boy from China? Please! Get real!

In early fall, we finally did get "the call." It was our agency on the line informing me that we had been referred a... boy! Not only was he a boy, but he was "older than you expected, about 14 months old by the time you pick him up in China." The words were from my dream, almost verbatim!

"What do you think?" asked the voice on the other end of the telephone.

I couldn't think. My hearing shut down. I thought I was going to faint. We had friends visiting from out of town, but my husband said, right in front of them, "You must be a witch! How could you have known that?"

Naturally, we accepted and love our wonderful son. I now feel the dream was God's way of letting me know we were getting a boy. I was given a glimpse into things that were to come in order to prepare me. I needed my thinking opened to the possibility of a boy!

The moral of my story is: don't barter, pay for, or work off a mural for a girl's room, such as, say... a garden scene, if there is any possibility (even one that you haven't exactly accepted) you might be referred a boy instead of a girl! My husband did suggest painting a hunter that could shoot the birds from the trees, but that's another story.

I have not had any more dreams foretelling the future. I truly believe this one dream was heaven sent to prepare me for my son, but if I dream about any numbers, you may one day be reading about me in the lottery section.

One more thing – although the only dreams involved were those that came true, our son does now have little sisters.

Hard Labor Creek

When our dossier went to China, the estimated wait was a very short time compared to these days. We were the types that bought nothing for our new daughter during those first months of the wait. We were "good" waiting parents. We never called the agency. We never worried. We knew that our day would come.

However, at the end of months and months of waiting, we started to get anxious. We thought our referral would come any day. We picked up some furniture for the nursery, bought a few things at yard sales, and talked about traveling to China.

A month later we were still waiting and getting very anxious at this point. Still, being good troopers, we did not call and harass the agency. We did carpet the nursery and buy a few books and toys we hoped would be a good match for our match – when it came!

As more time passed, our nerves were getting completely shot. Feeling that the stress had gotten the best of us, we took off late on a Friday afternoon for a weekend of camping. We planned to join friends in a nice, peaceful campground, complete with a beautiful lake and a comfortable breeze. Each of us took the newspapers we hadn't gotten to, along with a good book.

We had a delightful and stress-free Friday evening. We ate well and did a little hiking. Saturday morning, we were sitting in lawn chairs, reading, after a wonderful breakfast. Our friend looked up from her reading and said, "That looks like Aime's van." Sure enough, it did look like our mutual friend's van.

"Yes," I replied, but then immediately went back to my newspaper. Thirty seconds later, my friend exclaimed, "That is Aime's van!" To our amazement, the door opened and out popped Aime.

Now, this wouldn't have been so remarkable except that we hadn't told anyone where we were going. Well, that isn't quite true. Aime had invited us to dinner and we had to decline because we were going camping. She'd asked where, and we mentioned Hard Labor Creek. (The irony of the creek's name does not escape me.)

Our agency representative had been trying to reach us with our referral call since early evening on Friday. When we couldn't be found, she was relentless in her efforts. Eventually, she even contacted the references from our original adoption application. Aime was one of those references, so it was actually Aime who got "the call." Early Saturday morning, after searching the campground for more than an hour, it was Aime who found us and informed us that we had our referral!

The written referral information had been overnighted to Amie and was due to be delivered later that day. We made it back to civilization just as Aime received our package. Inside was our daughter's picture. She was, and still is, the most beautiful girl in our world. And the camping trip to Hard Labor Creek certainly remains the most memorable one of our lives!

GOD'S TIMING

Some days it was hard to believe that we had been waiting for years for a child. It got to the point where friends and family didn't even bother asking about the adoption. That made me sad, but I was also glad not to have to try to answer questions when I had no real answers. Nobody did.

Deciding to move to the special needs program was not a decision we took lightly. We called the agency and received lists of people who had adopted special needs. We talked to dozens of couples about their experiences. Mostly, we talked to the mothers, but sometimes the men would talk to each other, and that helped my husband to sort through which special needs he felt he could manage.

We sent in a medical checklist, but the agency told us that because of the narrow age range we were open to, it was going to be quite a while before we could expect to see information on possible matches. We were okay with that. We wanted a fairly young child with a minor special need condition, and we reasoned that the wait for that could never get as long as the wait we had already endured. We trusted in God's timing for us.

One month after turning in our checklist, we were contacted by our agency. They had a possible match for us! The truth is that we were not prepared for such a quick timeframe. We had not begun to set up the doctors and specialists we needed to review her file. We hadn't told our social worker we were going to move to the special needs program. We knew our immigration paperwork was expired. We hadn't even begun the newly required parent training. It was all just so fast, which seems like a weird thing to say after all those years of waiting.

I told my husband that I didn't think we should let the agency send the documentation, but he said that if we had trusted God's timing before, we should trust it now. We received the file on a darling little girl with a minor special need. The agency was adamant that we have the file assessed by "medical professionals" but there just wasn't time to locate the necessary specialists. We did ask our social worker to look over the file for developmental issues and had our own doctor look at the file. These were the only experts available to us and both of them said that the information looked good. Less than 48 hours after receiving the documentation, we accepted the child who would become our daughter.

It had been so many years and we were so excited that it was hard to wait while we completed training, new rounds of paperwork, and all the travel preparations. I was more than a little unhappy when I learned that, like everything else in the adoption process, the time between match and travel had lengthened. A lot.

And then the day came when we were handed this beautiful little girl. At that moment, I understood God's timing. No other time and no other child could have been so perfect for us.

IN SPIRIT

It was a Friday, and most of the people in our building (my husband worked at the same company) were gone for the weekend. I was alone in the office. Since I really wasn't in the mood to work, I thought of going home early, too, but sometime around 2 p.m., my phone rang. The adoption agency's representative on the other end introduced herself and I immediately asked her if this was "the call."

"Yes," she said, "This is it!"

I was shaking and crying so badly, I didn't remember to ask many questions, but I did manage to get that my daughter had just had her first birthday and was healthy. They said I could come to the agency that day or after the weekend to pick up the picture and sign the acceptance papers for the baby. I said I'd be there within the hour – I couldn't possibly wait over the weekend!

Our plan was that if I received "the call," I'd page my husband, Calvin. I wouldn't page him otherwise. When my page came through, he was in a meeting with a co-worker. He saw my number, jumped up, and explained he had to go because we'd just had a baby! He called me and started asking all the right questions – the ones I had forgotten to ask, the ones for which I didn't have answers. I remember him asking about her birthday, weight, age, when we'd go get her, and in typical Calvin style, "How much money do we bring?"

"Who cares? We have a daughter waiting for us!" We went to the agency and there, in the tiniest picture I'd ever seen, was the most beautiful baby in the world. After signing the papers, we stopped and purchased some celebratory champagne.

Calvin started making calls. One of those calls was to his best friend, who would eventually become our daughter's godfather. He came over to see her picture. He smiled and said, "It's really amazing that we both have the same birthday!"

I'm now in the waiting stage for a second child and looking forward to "the call." This time, I'll be sharing it with our daughter alone. Sadly, my husband passed away from a brain tumor. I wish that he was here to share the joy again, but I know his spirit is with us.

with an Audience

We really had no idea when our referral would come. One morning, my pager went off at work. Most of my pages at work were internal calls, so I was surprised to see an 800 number on the screen. Suddenly, it dawned on me that I had seen that number before... on our adoption agency's letterhead!

I ran to my cubical and looked up our agency's web page. Sure enough, the phone number matched. I was beyond shocked! I just knew it was "the call." My husband worked at the same company, so I called him to come to my cube. I wanted us to get the news together.

When he came to the phone, all I could manage to say was "Baby! Now! Come!" Luckily, my husband speaks gibberish, so he said he'd be right over. He turned to his co-workers and told them he had to go because he was about to become a father!

When he got to my cube, we called our agency and put the call on the speaker so we both could hear. We listened to the details about our daughter. We were so shocked we couldn't remember the questions we were supposed to ask. We just kept smiling and crying and writing things down.

Our family coordinator asked us for a fax number so she could fax the medical reports and a picture to us right away. I couldn't remember the number, but when I started to look it up, six people who had been eavesdropping around my cube suddenly started shouting out the number. We hadn't even realized anyone had been listening! So, we happily received the news of our daughter with a very large and enthusiastic audience.

oh no, you're not!

I admit it. I was cranky. At some point, as the time between dossier-to-China and referral kept lengthening, I had crossed over the line. I was more than cranky. Cross would be a kind word to describe my mood, and cantankerous would be a lightweight description of my demeanor. I was moving toward downright confrontational at an alarming speed. This, I'm sure, was duly noted by my agency.

I began calling them frequently. Well... more like daily, but I've heard that there were other in-process parents who called several times a day. Each morning, I'd put in a call. I'd listen to the careful answers of the agency representative and then hang up in a dark mood. I'm sure there were people in my office that wondered how I managed to keep a storm cloud hanging above my head indoors, month after month.

On the morning I finally received my match, I managed to get through to the agency just as they opened their phone lines – a few minutes late due to a snowstorm. The receptionist explained that only one agency representative had made it into the office at that point, and she wasn't my usual contact. I didn't care. I just wanted to hear somebody, any-body, tell me something!

The voice on the other end of the line was light and cheery – some-thing I was in no mood for. She explained that matches were on their way, but unfortunately, the agency did not yet know which groups had been included.

"You know we'll contact you the moment we have news," she tried to assure me. We talked about ways to control the anxiety. We talked about how it would "all be worth it, someday." We even talked about the weather, since their storm had been our storm two days earlier. I hung up feeling a little better, but still dissatisfied.

Just as I was leaving for lunch, my line rang without going through my secretary. This wasn't unusual, but it did make my heart skip a beat. I picked up the phone and heard, "Hi, this is the agency."

For some reason, my reaction, which I immediately voiced, was "No, it's not!" I had lived in such a state of disbelief for so long I couldn't accept that this was going to be "the call."

"Really, it's the agency, and I have great news for you," she continued.

"No, it's not. I just spoke with the representative this morning and you don't sound anything like her!" I had no idea where that statement came from, but once the words were out there, I believed them.

From the other end of the line, there was a minute of total silence, followed by, "I don't know why I sound different, but it really is me, and this really is your referral call!"

I have no idea why I reacted the way I did, but I practically shouted into the phone, "This is not funny. I am in no mood for practical jokes!" I slammed down the receiver and just stood there – shaking.

A couple of minutes later, my secretary burst into my office, saying the agency was on the phone and they had instructed her to check on me. They were concerned that I might have had a heart attack or something!

I guess the appearance of my secretary brought me back to reality, because I picked up the phone just as I dissolved into tears. The representative, her voice tinged with genuine alarm, asked if I was okay. I tried to apologize for my strange behavior, but all I could really manage was crying.

She proceeded to give me the information on my perfect child, stopping every few minutes, to make sure I was actually writing the information down. By the end of the conversation, we were laughing and crying together.

That agency representative and I eventually became good friends. We talk frequently. I have never – not even once – since that day, failed to recognize her voice.

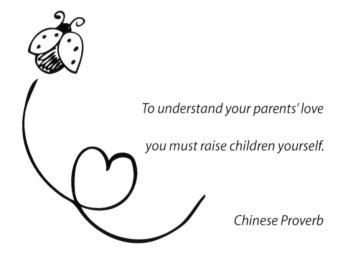

To understand your parents' love

you must raise children yourself.

Chinese Proverb

Not a Chance

While we were in the beginning stages of adopting from China, the program for adopting special needs children was undergoing many changes. We knew our daughter was waiting for us in China so these changes didn't deter us.

Unfortunately, the wait from the time your dossier arrived in China until referral was steadily increasing. Since daddy-to-be was in law school, we were trying to time our paperwork so that we would travel to China towards the end of his third, and final, year of school.

At about the time our paperwork was sent to China, I began running an Internet forum for families who were using the same agency as us. This was my constant source of information and helped me feel connected to the process. My husband, on the other hand, knew in his mind we wouldn't hear anything for more than a year and really didn't need much more information than that. I would try to pass information on to him on a regular basis, but he just kept reminding me that nothing was going to change for many, many months.

About six months after our dossier arrived in China, three months of dossiers for special needs families were processed within a one-month period. This was very exciting for me, although my husband simply discounted it by saying they would probably now skip a few months. He warned me not to get my hopes up. But, the next month they processed two more months of dossiers, so my reasoning was that at that point if they processed two months again, we could have a referral the next month! My husband continued to discount this information.

Through information on the forum and from the agency itself, I learned of a double referral batch. This meant we would be in the next batch! The wait was becoming unbearable, but the known really was so much better than the unknown, and it enabled me to settle in for the wait.

Just two days later, my secretary handed me a message from my agency contact. I try to calm down by reminding myself of the matches received just two days earlier. Obviously, it's just a call to update some information.

When I get my agency contact on the line, the first thing I hear is, "Are you sitting down?" I know what that means. Before she can even start speaking, I proceed to tell her that is not why she is calling me! I mention the referrals received just two days earlier. I jabber on about my not being in that batch, so that is not why she called me.

All the while, she's trying to explain that is exactly why she is calling me. By this point, I'm crying so hard I can hardly think of the questions I should ask. I manage to get some scant information, then I hang out in the back room for a solid 10 minutes trying to calm down enough to call my husband's office without the secretary thinking it was a bad emergency.

I'm not the only one in a state of disbelief. My husband is so stunned, all he can say is "You're kidding! You're kidding!" There are more stunned reactions as I spread the news throughout my office – hardly anyone had known about our adoption.

In the end, we received our referral months earlier than we'd anticipated. This meant we actually had to travel to China during the first two weeks of my husband's last year of law school. Missing the start of school is generally only excused for your own death. We were extremely lucky in that the dean of the law school was very understanding, as she had adopted the year before!

Answer the Phone

We were sitting in the kitchen having lunch when the phone rang. My wife jokingly said that since it wasn't for her, we should just let the voicemail answer it. I decided to go ahead and make the effort. The first thing I heard was, "Hi, this is the agency. I'm looking at a picture of your new daughter!" I get chills just saying it again!

What a shock! It was truly a "you'd better sit down for this" phone call. At the time of the call, no referrals had come in for a very long time. We had also resigned ourselves to at least another few weeks, because we knew the China Center of Adoption Affairs would be closing down for the Chinese New Year. As the representative tried to give me details, all I could repeat to her was "No way!" She kept answering, "It's true!"

Eventually, I told my wife to get on the other phone. Once again, the agency representative started giving us details and I quickly wrote down everything on the nearest piece of paper – the back of a junk mail envelope. When she said she'd just emailed the referral picture, we raced into the next room to open our email and then… we saw our little girl for the first time.

After immediately printing off the emailed version of the photo, we got ourselves ready for the hour-long drive to the agency. We placed our little darling's picture up on the dashboard as we somehow floated down the highway while I tried to keep my eyes on the road.

At the agency, we met with several people who showed us on a huge wall map of China exactly where our daughter was located. We received several differing interpretations of her Chinese name. We were given some information about what to expect regarding our travel – where we would go, and that it would be unlikely we visit the actual orphanage's city. We were also given four additional photos of our daughter. Even though her weight on the records was, as a renowned doctor would later tell us, "humanly impossible for her age," we signed the acceptance letter right then and there! Finally, we took a few photos with our agency representative before we left the office. From that day on, whenever I spoke to her, I always called her "Auntie" for her role in the birth of our family.

After we left the agency, we stopped at a nearby Chinese restaurant. The tiny picture was placed in the middle of the table, leaning against a salt shaker, for our first family meal together. When we noticed the waitress looking at the picture, we told her what had happened that day. She was very happy for us. She brought a few other restraunt employees over and showed them our picture and the characters of her name. Once again, everyone seemed to have a different interpretation of what her name meant!

We spent the rest of that wonderful day happily calling relatives and friends with the news: our daughter was on her way. And the name issue was resolved long before she arrived home.

They will wait

That August brought a phone call that changed my life forever. Our agency had said the day before that referrals were on their way, but probably would not arrive for a few days. So, we spent that day at a golf tournament, carrying and keeping our "personal communication device" on silent during the entire event just in case, even though they were forbidden by the tournament. (Psst... don't tell!) There was *no way* we were going to miss *that* call!

The day came and went with no phone call, just as our agency representative had predicted. On the morning of what turned out to be our Match Day, I was expecting my best friend and her daughter to arrive at the local airport. I'd told myself I would wait at home until an hour before their scheduled landing before heading out the door. About a half hour before I was supposed to leave, another friend called to tell me she'd gotten "the call" about her own beautiful daughter! My heart started pounding. I paced the house, waiting until time to go, when I'd have to force myself to leave.

Just then, the phone rang. I jumped up and checked the caller ID. The agency! I took a breath and answered the phone.

Finally – it really was "the call" we'd been waiting for! Our social worker was on the line!

"Hi," she said, "it's Bridget, from the agency."

"Uh... huh," I stammered.

"You are home!"

"Uh... huh," I stammered again.

"You're waiting on some information from us," she said with a laugh in her voice. I finally managed to get out a *yes*.

"I have the information you want," she said, "Your daughter –"

With those two little words, I started to cry. My hands reached for a pen and paper. I started writing the name of my daughter. My daughter, the one I'd been waiting for forever!

Bridget told me her name and birth date, then asked when I'd be coming to the agency. I explained that I had to go to the airport to pick up my best friend and her daughter. We'd be there as fast as possible. She ended the conversation by letting me know that wasn't a problem. My daughter would be waiting for us.

I called my husband and cried, "We have a baby! I have to go to the airport!" Hearing all the details, he got as excited as I was. He asked if I was okay to drive. I laughed through my tears and told him I was fine, and I'd let him know when I left the airport. By this time, it was long past time to go. I was going to be late. I didn't care. I knew my friends would be waiting for me and would be more than happy to know the reason for my delay.

Not-So-Instant communication

Friday the 13th brought the news that China had been awarded the Olympics. This was nice news, but I'd been waiting all week for "the call" that I had been told might come later in the week.

I wouldn't even allow my 16-year-old to get online because we had only the one phone line, and I didn't want to miss anything. Fortunately, he's a very laid back teen and he was agreeable. When it got to be 7 p.m., I realized our agency office had to be closed.

"I'm going stir crazy!" I announced. I'd been housebound all week, just waiting for "the call." We headed out.

We got home again at 9:15 p.m. As I was putting my purse and keys away, my son asked, "So, can I go online now, Mom?" I nodded my agreement and said sadly, "I don't think anyone will be calling this late before a weekend."

He sat down at the computer, but soon complained that he couldn't get online. "Mom, do you have a message in your voicemail?" I checked. Sure enough, the automatic beep that indicated I had a message was firing away. It was a message from our agency representative!

She'd called at 9:10 p.m. to tell me she had a little girl for me. I immediately hung up the phone – without properly exiting the voicemail – and tried to call the agency. I got the after-hours answering machine so I left a message. Wondering if the agency would try to email me the information, I then tried to get online, but it still didn't seem to be working. I lifted the receiver. Once again, I heard the beep indicating another message.

Thinking this was because I hadn't exited voicemail correctly, I hesitated before checking for another message. Yes! There was! While I was feverishly calling and trying to access my email, the agency representative had left a second message at 9:22 p.m. She said she knew I couldn't go through the weekend without the information, so she was emailing it to me. It took a few minutes, then there it was – my daughter's picture and information right there on my screen.

I would later learn that a dear friend adopting from the same program had actually received a phone call from the agency representative that same night, regarding *my* referral. Somewhere, in the time span between her two calls to me, the representative had called her. Explaining that she was unable to reach me, the representative wanted my friend's opinion on whether she should email the photo or not.

When told, "Send the photo! Send the photo!" that's exactly what she did.

So goes my story of "the call" – or I should say, two incoming calls, two outgoing calls, an agency representative's call to a friend of mine, and finally, the appearance of my darling daughter on my computer screen!

I Saw Brother Kissing...

To say that our 14-year-old biological son was less than thrilled when we decided to adopt would be putting it mildly. He was really upset. He'd ruled the roost his entire life, had his parents all to himself, and was basically a spoiled teen.

He pointed out, in the melodramatic speech of a teenager, that the entire situation would be grossly embarrassing to him. Not only were we too old for a baby, but we were also adopting from a foreign country. He said he'd never be able to show his face in this town ever again! Never! Never, never again!

Though many people found the lengthening time frames unbearable, for us, it was a blessing. The longer it took for the entire process, the longer our son had to get used to the idea. We knew he had a heart of gold and would eventually come around, but he needed time.

During the wait, we began to participate in some of the China culture functions available in our area. We went to the Chinese New Year's celebrations, dragging a decidedly sullen son with us. We visited the local Chinese cultural school – where he at least showed an interest in the computer programs. We visited with other families who'd completed their adoptions – and he made it quite clear he found the outings boring and a complete waste of his time.

A couple of months before our anticipated referral date, we sat down with him. We told him that we felt like he wasn't warming up to the idea and we were growing more and more concerned. We needed to begin making some basic travel plans and we wanted to know if he was planning to accompany us to China. He said he had no intention of going to China, even if it meant staying home with his aunt. He was referring to my sister. She and my son had clashed since his toddler days and for him to volunteer to stay with her – that told us just how much he really still disliked our decision. We were genuinely worried.

On the day that "the call" came, I was sick. I'd called in from work because I was too ill to go in. My head ached, my nose was stuffy, and I was coughing like a barking seal. I wasn't in a very good mood, to say the least. But when I heard those magic words, *you have a daughter*, I did what most new mommies do – cry with joy.

I decided to use the good news as an excuse to get my husband to come home. I called his office and told him I really wasn't feeling well and that he needed to come home. I didn't let on that we'd received our referral. He tried to argue against it, but I was adamant.

By the time he arrived, I had our daughter's emailed picture up on our computer screen. He was surprised to find me in the office, rather than confined to bed, but forgave me for the deception once he saw her little face on the screen. We were laughing, crying, and celebrating when our son walked in.

"This is your little sister," I said, as I backed away from the computer.

"She's cuter than I thought she would be." He said, before immediately leaving for ball practice.

We weren't sure if his reaction had been negative or positive, but at least he hadn't run screaming from the house. We were happy with that much. We decided to wait to see how any further reactions developed, now that she was "real" and not just a vague concept.

Later that night, I found I just couldn't sleep. It was all too exciting. I wandered downstairs to the office, where we had printed off several pictures of our daughter. I nearly walked in on my son, but saw him in time and was able to peek at him from the other side of the door.

"Well, Peanut," he said, speaking to the picture, "I guess you're gonna be my little sister, after all. It's going to be just fine." Then I watched as he picked up the photograph and gave "Peanut" a quick kiss.

Everything turned out far better than "just fine." Now away at college, our son says he can't imagine what life was like without his little sister. When he's away from her, he really misses her — we have the phone bills to prove it. And to this day, she's still his "Peanut."

A single tree cannot

make a forest.

Chinese Proverb

Family and Friends

We knew the referrals had finally arrived. My husband and I knew the information on our newest little one, our second daughter, was in the hands of the trustworthy telephone stork.

Instead of laboring on a bed, watching monitors and checking the baby's heart rate, we paced together, back and forth from the den to the kitchen, from the kitchen to the den, checking the phone line, making sure it was clear, taking deep breaths to calm ourselves. All done in anticipation of "the call." *You know if you look at your phone hard enough, long enough, it will ring.*

We were not in this alone. The submission of our paperwork was timed to be in conjunction with the paperwork of our good friends. Our agency gladly sent our dossiers to China at the same time, with hopes that our families would receive our matches together and we would be able to travel with each other to pick up our daughters.

A few times, I braved a call to my friend. "Did you hear anything yet?"

"No, what about you?"

We quickly hung up so as not to tie up our phone lines. Then, in two homes, four parents resumed their pacing, waiting, and watching the phone.

Finally, in the middle of the afternoon, a call came in. My husband and I answered the phone together – one of us in the kitchen, the other in the den. The pacing stopped. Our hearts were the only things that needed monitoring now, as we soaked in the information from our telephone stork.

The words fluttered in. Our little one was a healthy 12-month-old. They would email a picture of her to our neighbor because our computer was down. I asked if my friends had gotten their referral.

"I can't give out that information," the adoption agency stork said.

I explained that we had timed our paperwork to go together and I didn't want to know any details. I added how we had planned to go out to eat together to celebrate that night and I really would like to know so we can make plans. I was asked to hold for a moment. I could hear the rustling of papers and the movement of a chair.

"We are working through all the referrals, and yes, your friends received their referral, but they haven't been contacted yet."

Yes! We were excited to say the least. Our neighbors called us and told us to come over to see the picture of our new daughter. So we, along with our four-year-old daughter, hustled over there, camera in hand. They welcomed us into their home and escorted us straight to the computer. There she was... a little bald-headed, round-faced angel, sitting in a walker.

"Look, look!" I told my daughter, "That's your new baby sister!" She smiled. She'd waited so long to have a sister. Sometimes she wondered if it was ever really going to happen. Finally, she could see her, and she was very happy.

What about our friends? Do they know anything yet? We returned home, and I braved another call to them. "Well, any news?" I nervously asked.

"No, nothing! What about you?"

"Yes! We got the call!" I filled her in. It was hard not to tell her that I knew their referral was in, but I knew they had to hear it from the agency.

After hanging up, we resumed pacing. This time, it was on behalf of our friends. Finally they called – they had their referral! Their daughter was in a different province than ours, but our referrals were both in. We were all thrilled!

We met that night at a Chinese restaurant. We shared the photos we'd printed of our new daughters and celebrated in style. It was a few days before Christmas. We couldn't have asked for a better Christmas present than this!

Sharing that second adoption with our best friends was so special for us. While we didn't travel together the whole trip, we did spend some time together in Guangzhou, both meeting each other's daughters for the first time halfway around the world.

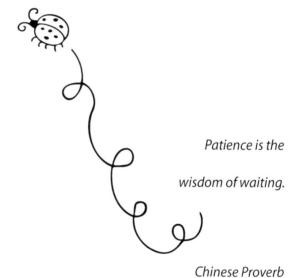

Patience is the

wisdom of waiting.

Chinese Proverb

Up to Date

When we first started the adoption process, people were getting their children within a couple years. I watched as the time to Match Day got longer and longer but was reassured that it would never get to four years. Heck, the director of our agency had told a bunch of us in a special meeting for families who were waiting that they believed the wait would never reach four years.

Those years came and went. And then another. And another. It looked to me like we would finally get matched in our seventh year. SEVEN YEARS! If we had been told that at the beginning, we would have walked away. Actually, we were told that, but by a domestic agency, so that is why we looked to China. A couple of years didn't seem so bad in comparison.

Like everybody else, we had a lot of frustration, but there really wasn't anything to be done, so we tried to just get on with our lives. Every once in a while, a family member or friend would check in. The questions went from "When will you get your daughter?" to "Are you guys still adopting?" Those questions and those days were painful. It didn't surprise me that so many thought we had given up on the idea. Though we never spoke about it, I felt like each of us had given up. We just couldn't bring ourselves to say it out loud.

A few months before what looked to be our Match Day, our agency started calling and sending emails regarding getting our home study updated. We had long ago stopped reacting quickly to their requests. After all, this many years in, what did a few weeks or even a few months matter? We never did update.

We have to admit now that the agency thoroughly explained that by being so nonchalant about the updates, we were likely to delay our travel, once the match did happen. I guess since we had kind of stopped believing in the match, we had also kind of stopped believing in what the agency had to say.

Then it happened. The phone in my office rang and on the other end was a woman I had talked to hundred of times. "It's your match call," she began, "I am looking at a picture of your daughter!"

I had expected to be excited. I had expected to cry. Instead, I was just very quiet and methodical as I took down information to share later with my husband. After she got through most of the statistical information, she said, "I am emailing you her picture right now. Just let me know when you receive it."

I was surprised to see it come so quickly – just a matter of seconds. I opened the attachment and suddenly a switch was flipped. I was looking at a picture of my dream-come-true! "OMG! OMG! OMG!" I yelled through my tears. (Literally O-M-G, having long ago adopted the acronyms associated with instant messaging as part of my normal speech.)

Both of the secretaries burst into my office to find me a sobbing, disheveled mess, still mumbling those three letters. They saw the picture on the computer and got a little teary-eyed themselves. One of them took the phone and let the agency know I had received the picture and was, or would be, just fine.

Once I shared the news with my husband, we waited excitedly for the overnight package with the documents and got started right away on our updates. Unfortunately, our agency was right. Because our paperwork was out of date, it was a couple extra months before we could travel. If I thought waiting for the match was hard, waiting for travel was *killer*. We are in process for a second child now. You can bet our paperwork is up to date at all times!

What A woman wants

Let me just say that I am the dad. My wife said I should tell our story because I was the one "with the story." I don't see it that way. I loved – love – my wife. I wanted – want – her to have everything that she wants. And what she wanted was our child.

The matches were due. We knew that from the online adoption forums. I told my wife to go ahead and take "the call" when it came. She could then relay the information to me. After all, she had been waiting for "the call" for years in a way I never understood.

I went to work and she waited at the house. About lunch time I called and she didn't answer, which I thought was pretty weird, but then I wondered if she was actually on the call with the agency. When I hadn't heard from her by middle of the afternoon, I tried her again. There was still no answer and I was getting worried.

About then, my secretary announced that the agency was on the phone. It was "the call." They told me they had been trying to reach my home all day, but nobody answered. They gave me all the information about our daughter, and emailed me the picture. That child was *beautiful*, if I do say so myself!

I tried calling home again, and when there was no answer, I decided to head out, but not before printing off the information and the photo about 10 times over. It was a weird feeling to be so happy and so worried at the same time.

210 / ladybug love

When I reached the driveway and could see my wife's car, I got scared. What if something had happened to her on this day, of all days? I hit the back door calling her name and running. And I hit the floor hard! In her nervous energy, my wife had waxed and buffed the kitchen floor, which I promptly slipped on.

They tell me I was unconscious for the better part of 15 minutes and as I was coming to, I kept mumbling. The paramedics seemed to get a real kick out of my ranting. Apparently, "I have what you want more than anything else in the world! In the car! Baby!" is some kind of double entendre when a man is barely conscious!

It was several more minutes before my wife came to understand that I had received "the call" and the information on our child was in my car. The paramedics were a little confused as she left my side and ran out to my car. I was pretty sure I was okay, but once my wife had her hands on that picture she started crying so hard, the paramedics insisted both of us go to the hospital to be checked out. (Apparently, they can't tell tears of joy from tears of pain.)

We still don't know what happened with the phone, but I have remained very proud of the fact that unconscious or not, I knew what my woman wanted. Still do. She just put the application for our second child in front of me.

It Goes Both Ways

We knew of several families that had originally wanted a healthy child but then opened their homes to a special needs child. It all seemed to be going well for them, but we did wonder if everyone was really open to special needs, or if the faster time to a child match influenced the decisions. In the end, it didn't seem to matter because those kids and their families were so happy!

We knew about James 1:27, but as our church explored orphan ministry we learned of so many other instances in the Bible – so many we had never even noticed – where the more fortunate are called upon to assist orphans.

We felt like we were called to adopt a child. It seemed to us that a child with special needs could use our help the most. So, we came to the China adoption process with the intention of adopting a special needs child.

We wanted to rescue a child that might not otherwise get the opportunity for a loving home, so we deliberately looked at some of the more difficult needs. This was the opposite of what we saw most people doing. We found that fear grew in our heads, even as love grew in our hearts. It was not easy, but we eventually turned in the list of medical conditions.

This was all well and good in theory. We did not realize that because some children are harder to place than others, the agencies are always on the lookout for those willing to take on a bit more. When we got "the call" asking us to review documentation on a child that had what I considered the second most severe condition on our list, I absolutely panicked.

What had made me think we could take on a child with such a severe condition? Would our finances really withstand the medical bills? Even with insurance, our part of the bills could be thousands of dollars. What if we couldn't actually give this precious child the life we planned? We could give all the love in the world in our home, but she would have to go out into the big, bad world at some point. It scared me, but relying upon our faith, we accepted the child and started the final round of paperwork so that we could travel to China as soon as possible.

We've been home almost a year now, and it has sometimes been harder than I ever imagined, but not for the reasons I thought. Watching your young child being prepped for surgery will rip the heart right out you! But when she awoke from surgery, she wanted her mom. As I held her, being careful of airway filters, drainage tubes, and staples, I realized that we had rescued this child, but she had rescued us, too. Without her, we would have continued to exist, but never live, and we would never have come to know God's true grace. I can say without reservation that the rescue has gone both ways.

BIRthday fOR TWO

It's my birthday. My husband asks what I want for my birthday. I want my baby! My mom wonders what little something she can get me for my birthday. I want my baby! My sister gently inquires if there is something that I need for my birthday. I want my baby!

I take the day off – *because it's my birthday* – but I am so depressed, I don't want to go anywhere or do anything. In my plaid flannel pajamas, I watch a marathon of chick flicks and wish the phone would stop ringing. Thank you all very much for the birthday wishes, but I can't have the one thing I want for my birthday, so I just want to be left alone.

My cell rings again. I get up to go look at the screen so I can make a decision about answering or not. The agency number shows up with that silly little picture I made of their logo. I answer with a very slow hello – and begin to hold my breath.

"It's the agency, and we have great news for you!" the voice begins. There is a split second when I am crushed because I thought the first words I would hear would be that it is the match call, but then she continues, "I'm looking at a picture of your daughter!"

The air swooshes out of my lungs, and I try to gulp it back in, but I've begun sobbing so hard I just can't get the breathing thing right! The voice on the other end grows concerned. "Are you okay?"

I can't breathe. No, really, I can't breathe! There are a few moments of silence while I get myself under control, then I say something like "uhminute." The adoption agency angel waits patiently.

"Tell me." I manage, and she proceeds to give me a ton of information about my child. We are several minutes into the conversation, when it hits me.

"Did you say *today* is her first birthday?"

My daughter and I now share a special tradition. We dress in our matching flannel pajamas, watch movies, and turn the phone off to celebrate our birthday for two!

I TRIed to waRn you

I work from home. My house is a lodge I built deep in the woods a few years ago. One of the disadvantages of this is that I do have to rely on spotty old-fashioned landline telephone service. Cell phones will rarely work out here. One of the advantages of working from this beautiful place is that I can temporarily stop whatever project I am working on and run down to the basement to throw in a load of laundry. One morning, I was doing just that when I heard my guard dog going berserk upstairs.

I should tell you this was not all that unusual, so I was not overly concerned. That puppy is about 140 pounds of what is commonly known as a large breed dog, which means he is the size of a small horse and has a bark that can be heard three counties away. Unfortunately, while he is very good at warning me of a stranger coming up the driveway, he is also prone to barking if a deer comes into the yard or, looking through the patio door, he spies a lizard scampering across the deck. You'll see why I mention this as you read my story.

Because it was broad daylight, I have a full alarm system, and frankly, because the dog is so sensitive, I chose to ignore him and continue folding my laundry. By the time the chore was completed, he had settled down so I didn't think anything more of it. I put the laundry away, poured another cup of coffee, and settled back into my office.

A couple hours later, the phone rang. It was the agency explaining that they had been trying to reach me since yesterday. I was completely

216 / ladybug love

shocked. Not only because I hadn't realized the phone had been temporarily out, again, but also because I had long ago stopped dreaming about my match call.

As the lovely woman began relaying the information about my daughter, I went into a daze. The whole thing was just so surreal. I was coaxed back to reality when she mentioned that, due to an upcoming holiday in China, there was a time crunch for getting the letters of acceptance back. Because of that, they had gone ahead and overnighted my daughter's information to me. It was supposed to arrive by 4:00 that afternoon.

Except that I knew the overnight delivery service only came out my way once per day and that was in the morning. In the morning – as in a couple hours ago – when my guard dog had temporarily lost his mind!

I asked the woman to hold on and flew through the living room to the front door. I nearly threw open the door, but stopped in time to punch in the alarm code. I was already a blubbering mess and puppy dog was already going crazy because of my crying and running. I didn't need to add a shrill alarm to the mix!

I yanked open the door and looked down to find the package at my feet. Scooping it up, I ran back to the phone. I tore into the package and was able to see several pictures of my precious girl as the agency representative continued with my long, long awaited match call. Of course, it was really hard to hear what she had to say because I had caused puppy to get overexcited and he barked through the remainder of "the call!"

Thank YOU, OfFICeR

It was exciting to know I was going to be matched the next morning. My agency had put out the word that matches were in and being translated. Calls would begin at 9:00 a.m. I called to ask if it would be okay to just be at their office waiting when they opened the doors, but they discouraged this. I was to wait until I received "the call," then I could hurry over.

Match Day dawned cold and gray. The weatherman had predicted snow but it hadn't arrived yet. I wasn't too worried. I'm a mountain girl and even a blizzard would not have prevented me from getting to the agency to get the information on my daughter!

It didn't occur to me that they would call the people on the East Coast first. I somehow had it in my head that since we were right there, we would get the first calls, but the minutes and then the hours on the clock ticked by. Finally, about two hours after the lunch that I had skipped for fear of missing the phone call, my assistant let me know the agency was on the line. I didn't know the person who called, but was instantly in love with anybody bringing this news to me! After a brief bit of information, she told me, "Come on in for the picture. She really is adorable!" I thanked her and told her I would be there within the hour.

When I got outside the building, I realized the weather had changed drastically during the morning. It was entirely possible we were going to have a blizzard after all, but I was determined to see my little girl.

I carefully drove out of our parking lot, maneuvered my way onto the cross street, and finally managed to get up the ramp to the freeway. It was there that I was promptly hit by a car sliding sideways across the road. It spun my car around a couple times, and I felt a surreal slow motion as my car began to flip onto its side.

Although it looked and felt dramatic, I really wasn't hurt and I really wanted to get to the agency. But there were other cars involved, people who were shook up, if not actually hurt, and a beehive of police and tow truck activity for the next couple hours. After being checked out by the paramedics, I was placed in the backseat of a police cruiser and told one of the officers would be along to take me home.

It seemed like forever until the policeman got into the car. By then I was cold, frustrated, and beginning to feel some soreness. I was also crying pretty hard, so when he worriedly asked me if I was okay, all I could get out was, "I want my baby!" Naturally, he became alarmed and tried to find out if I had a child in my car that everyone had missed! Seeing the concern on his face made me pull myself together.

I finally got the full explanation out. And then that wonderful policeman immediately drove me to the agency, where my match had been waiting for me for hours. I can never thank that officer enough!

Baby Blue

My husband and I had started the adoption process with such hope, but as the years rolled by, that hope faded until it couldn't even be seen or felt anymore. We discussed the situation and agreed that if we reached five years, we would just give up on the whole idea.

The five years came, so we talked it over with each other one last time and then reluctantly called the agency to say we were withdrawing. Like everything else to do with the adoption process, it turned out there was a specific procedure we had to follow to exit the process. We had to write a letter and that letter had to go to China, and, and, and...

We meant to take care of that. And we meant to return the messages from the agency. And we genuinely meant to stop the adoption, but life got busy. My husband got a new job, I was promoted, and we were both spending much more time in volunteer service for our church. We were also remodeling our house. The nursery had been sitting there empty for more than five years and it was time to let it go. I was incredibly sad as I took on the project of covering the pastel greens with a rather vibrant shade of blue.

I had just about finished painting what was going to be the new media room, when I heard the phone ring for about the fifth time that morning. I had ignored it while painting, but this time it had become too irritating, so I ran to answer.

It was our agency on the line, and we had a match! Not only that, but we had been matched with a boy! I was completely confused, but the agency representative explained that they had not been able to close our file without our express written instructions. All that time, we had still been in process. She also let me know that because we had not specified a gender in our letter to China, we were just as likely to receive a boy as a girl. I was flabbergasted and not at all sure what my next steps should be. The agency representative gently told me that we could still choose not to accept. I laughed and cried and assured her that we *would* be accepting!

When I hung up the phone, I realized I had to share this news with my husband, but how was I going to do that? There was no way to help him make sense of all this with his entire office watching. I dialed his number and through my tears said, "You have to come home, right now." He started to argue, but then realized there must be some serious emergency at the house. He hung up and was home within 15 minutes.

He found me painting the room blue, which was how he had left me a few hours earlier, except that now I was obviously much happier about the prospect. He looked scared, concerned and angry all at the same time.

"Do you really, really like this color?" I asked.

"What? *What?* You make me come home thinking there is some emergency to ask about *paint colors*? I knew this was going to be hard on you, but are you *completely nuts*?"

I kept smiling, but the tears were streaming down my face now. "It's baby blue," I told him, "and you have a son!"

He promptly fell onto the can of blue paint, and remained there, spellbound, as I explained the whole story. The paint soaked through the drop cloth, so that we had to paint even the floor blue. It suits the three of us just fine.

CHRISTMAS SISTER

Our daughter had been insisting for some time that she needed a sister. We knew it just wasn't meant to be. As youth pastors, we love our calling, but there just isn't a lot left at the end of the month, and adoptions aren't free.

During the month of December our daughter often accompanied us to the teen practices, Bible study, and decorating sessions. We were busy, so she would often play in the crèche area. At first, we were concerned that people might be offended by her playing with the crèche's baby Jesus doll, but we quickly found out people's hearts melted at the sight of a four-year-old holding a play cell phone to the doll's ear and chatting away in her pretend world.

One evening our meeting ran terribly late and we felt more than a little guilty when we found her curled up in the crèche, with the doll, cell phone, and purse tucked under her arm. We tried not to wake her up, but the minute we touched her she came to and said to us, "Baby Jesus called. He says we are getting a sister for next Christmas." Then she was out again.

We were worried because Christmas was fast approaching and we knew there was not going to be a sister. On Christmas, we were at the ready with distractions, explanations, hugs and whatever else we were going to need to keep her little heart from breaking. We were so surprised when she never said anything about a sister. Nothing at all. We decided to let it go, thinking that maybe she had been dreaming that night.

A few weeks after Christmas, she suddenly mentioned the sister idea again. As gently as possible, I tried to explain. "Oh, sweetie," I began. "Christmas was a few weeks ago. Don't you remember? Christmas has come and gone." She cocked her head and eyed me as if I was playing at being completely ignorant, "He said next Christmas, Mom."

In March, my husband sold some music he had been working on for years. It gave us enough to start the process. We put in a checklist with our agency. In June, our new church orphan ministry made us the first recipient of their grant. We also received and accepted the file of a darling little girl with a significant, but correctible, special need. We spent the summer and early fall doing every kind of fundraiser we could think of. By October, our agency began talking to us about travel and we were still a few thousand dollars short. We were getting worried. Then, when we needed it most, a grant that we had applied for months earlier came through. We couldn't believe it, but we were finally ready!

In December, as we prepared for travel, I asked our daughter what she wanted to take as an early Christmas present for her little sister. She insisted upon a play cell phone. When I asked why, she replied in that same eerily confident tone I'd heard once before, "So Baby Jesus can call her like He called me."

We got the hint. We've already put in another special needs checklist and begun the fundraisers for another sister.

Quite a Catch!

A few years ago my husband got a big kick out of a certain country song that basically implied that a man loved his wife, but not more than he loved fishing. One day the man had to choose. He chose fishing. I was not as amused by the song as he was, but my man loves fishing, so for him there was some legitimate connection to the song. When I say he loves fishing, well, let me explain it this way. After we had been dating for about a year, this was a man that, on a date, asked me to bait his hook for him. When I started to do so, I found my engagement ring tied to the line!

We used to joke that between fishing and our adoption process, my husband was going to be able to perfect patience. Me? Not so much. I hated that the process was going so slowly, and I hated when my husband would leave me alone for an entire day out of most weekends so that he could join his fishing buddies. I voiced my frustrations on more than one occasion, but I realized there was nothing I could do about the adoption timeline, and even less I could do about a Georgia boy who had been fishing almost from the time he could walk.

When the match call finally came, my husband was – you guessed it – fishing. It was actually a holiday weekend, and though I knew the matches were in, it didn't occur to me that the people at the agency would actually take a day in their weekend to do match calls, so I told my husband it was fine to go.

It was the sweetest thing I ever heard – listening to the information about our tiny daughter. When the email came through I was immediately in love with this petite little child with the determined eyes. I couldn't wait to share my joy with her daddy, but he wasn't reachable out on the river. I decided to have a little fun with the match.

We live just down the road from a sports store, so I went and purchased a certain fishing pole that my husband had been eyeing. Back at home, I carefully balanced the pole over the back of the sofa in the den, so that when he walked in, all he could see was the pole, and not the picture of our daughter that I had printed out and attached.

When he arrived home, I was bursting with the news, but was dissuaded from getting too crazy. After ten hours fishing in the sun, the first thing the man needed was a shower! When he finally came downstairs, he asked about my day. I gave him my most mischievous grin, telling him that I had done a little shopping. He didn't pick up on my hint. Instead, he rolled his eyes and said, "This kid's going to have more clothes than the mall!"

"That may be true, but I actually did a little shopping for you today. Let's go look in the den."

The minute we walked in the room, he recognized the fishing pole. He looked at me with eyes as big as saucers. Never in the history of our marriage had I actively encouraged his fishing obsession!

"You ain't seen nothing yet. I already baited a hook for you. It's going to get you the best catch ever!"

He stared at me, his eyes a mixture of curiosity and confusion. Then he saw the picture. When our eyes met again, they were filled with tears.

Our daughter has been home for several years now. Her daddy nicknamed her "Pole" and everybody seems to assume it's because she is a long, lean kid. We know the truth – it's all about the best catch of our lives.

Definitions

We came into the China adoption process just as the timelines began to grow exponentially. Our agency warned us that they had no idea what the future would bring, but somehow, in our own minds we invented what we thought a reasonable timeline was going to be. When that imaginary deadline passed, we grew very frustrated, very quickly. We knew it wasn't the agency's fault. We were the ones who picked the imaginary date, in spite of everything the agency said and the growing mountain of evidence saying the timelines were going to keep expanding. Knowing all that in our heads did nothing to soothe our hearts.

As part of trying to stay connected, once a month a large group of families would get together in our city. Some were waiting like us, but each month usually brought a new child or two. It helped us to see that kids were still coming home and families were still being grown by adoption. As time went on, we did notice that more and more special needs children were coming home. Some of the special needs were a little scary, but as the months passed, we watched as cleft lips were repaired, clubfeet were cast, and missing limbs replaced with prosthetics. After a while, we realized that we hadn't been afraid of special needs. We had just been afraid of the unknown. We had defined special needs one way, but the reality was something completely different.

We decided to put in a checklist with our agency. We called and talked to the special needs department. We were shocked to learn that because our dossier had already been in China for years *and* we were open to a number of conditions *and* we were open to a boy *and* to a child up to three years old, it was likely that we would begin receiving files to review pretty quickly.

Their definition of "pretty quickly" turned out to be the very next day! First, we received a phone call asking if we would consider the file of a child that fit well within the parameters we had on the checklist. This was followed by an email containing the file of a little two-year-old boy with a condition we were very familiar with. In addition to all the medical information and pictures, there was a short video. It was blatant in that video that his special need was not slowing him down at all.

He's been home almost a year now. He is the definition of "all boy" and our family is now the definition of "all joy!"

Hello, Kitty!

Waiting for our daughter was difficult for us, but we were not panicked like some of the other people we knew who were waiting. We had three active boys at home already, so our days were full. I'm the practical one in the household, so I explained it wasn't reasonable to spend money until closer to the adoption date, whenever that was going to be. Once in a while I would catch my wife buying a little pink pretty for the future daughter, but she didn't seem to be going overboard. There were a few things in the closet, but we didn't set up the nursery.

My wife was in charge of the paperwork, so I can't even tell you how many years passed, but I know I dutifully signed checks and periodically visited with our social worker. After a while, it got to be ludicrous. When we started, our boys were in elementary school, and now we had one headed for high school.

I tried to convince my wife that we were getting too old, that there was going to be too big an age gap, that we didn't want to start over with diapers again this late in the game. My wife wasn't buying it. She had longed for a daughter for years and she was willing to wait until that magical day happened. Period.

Finally, "the call" came in! I wasn't home. In fact, I was traveling overseas on business, and would not actually get home for about a week after the call, but my wife's adoption angel told her all the exciting information and emailed her a picture of a sweet-faced little girl. When my wife contacted me with the news, I was happy, but not as excited as I thought I would be. Maybe it was receiving the news so far from home. Maybe it had just been too long in coming. Whatever the reason, I didn't think we would be celebrating at the level I had originally anticipated.

When I returned home, my wife informed me that she had gone ahead and decorated the nursery. That was an understatement! She had painted the walls, ceiling, and floor an amazing pink color and bought every kitty-themed item every made! The room was a pink palace of girly stuff. Frankly, it made me nervous.

I just checked on our little sleeping Kitty before sitting down to write this. I nicknamed her that even before we brought her home, even though it has nothing to do with her given name. Can you guess why? She is in pink pajamas sleeping on pink sheets in the pink palace. It doesn't make me nervous at all anymore. I 've never seen anything so beautiful in my life.

Namesake

It was hard to face. After ten years of marriage, there were still no babies, so we tried the IVF route. Four times. Four fails. We talked about a surrogate mother, but in the end neither of us was comfortable with that choice. We looked at adoption, but domestic adoption seemed fraught with pitfalls. We were slowly, sadly coming to the conclusion that there wasn't going to be a baby story for us, not even through adoption.

One afternoon, two or three years after we had basically given up on adopting, we were at the park with our dogs when a lovely blonde woman entered the playground. She had two Asian children with her. We were curious, but didn't want to intrude, so we hung back just a little. We were amazed when each of the girls shouted, "Mommy, come help me!" to the blonde. This took it from a passing curiosity to full-on intrigue. We just had to ask. The woman was very gracious and explained that she had adopted from China. Twice. She suggested that we contact her agency, which we did.

Once more, it seemed like our dream of a family was going to be thwarted. The agency explained that the China adoption timeline had extended out so far that they were no longer taking applications for what they called the "regular" program. Our curiosity was peaked again. If there was a regular program, what was the irregular program?

We requested and received a huge amount of information about the special needs adoptions and decided we would be just fine with a minor correctible need. We put in a checklist. We knew there were a few others ahead of us who had requested the same special needs, so we knew it would be a while. What we didn't expect was that more than a year would pass.

We were very discouraged and when it came time for us to re-new our immigration, we really didn't want to do it. Our agency told us that it was their policy that we keep our documentation current, or they would not be able to search the list for the right match for us. We felt like we were being held hostage, but we made the required appointment with our social worker.

She was coming on a Tuesday evening. We really liked her. In fact, she had gone way beyond the call of duty, and spent extra hours in visits with us. She had talked us off the ledge more than a few times. We had become friends.

She arrived a few minutes early, but thanks to my "day off" the place was sparkling, I was showered and dressed appropriately, and fresh-squeezed lemonade was in the refrigerator. I might not have wanted the meeting, but our social worker was never going to know it!

My husband came in a few minutes later and the visit officially began. We were about ten minutes in, when the home phone rang. We chose to ignore it, but a few minutes later, my cell phone rang, too. I apologized, and quickly ran to turn it off. When I saw that it was the agency, I answered instead. They had a file for us to review! They wanted to email it right then and there!

Our social worker suggested we take our laptop into the family room so that the two of us could look at the file without her intrusion, but we were having none of that. This might be our child, but she had played a very big role in helping us get to this point. We were just fine sharing with her.

As the pictures came up on the screen, the three of us gasped at the same time. This child was exquisite! We were all a little confused as to the special need because it was not immediately evident. We turned to the video, which helped us to see the issue, but it appeared so minor. We were smitten! Our social worker told us she understood our emotions, but she strongly encouraged us to have the file reviewed by the pediatrician we had selected before making a final decision. We promised we would.

In some ways, it was hard to continue the meeting, but in others, it made it so much easier. Now there was a reason to listen and learn. We were talking about a child, a specific child (no matter what we told each other, we all knew this was our baby) and we needed to be as prepared as possible for what was coming.

A few months later we brought our daughter home. Our social worker was very pleased when she learned we named our little girl after her!

Good heart,

good reward.

Chinese Proverb

A LITTLE BLUE BOX

When we married, I brought some of the Christmas traditions from my childhood to my new home and family. One of those was that Santa brought his Christmas presents while we slept early Christmas morning. The other was that during the month of December, gifts would be placed under the tree as they came in; packages from grandparents, brother to sister gifts, mom to daughter gifts, and the like. On Christmas Eve, each family member got to open one gift from any other family member. Even though it was just me and my husband, I insisted that we continue this, so for the first few years of our marriage, it seemed like I opened a package of socks several years in a row!

While we were in process, Christmases were hard. I remember thinking year after year that next Christmas would be different, but it never was. I think my husband sensed my annual misery, because the gifts I got to open became more and more extravagant.

One Christmas Eve, I was pretty low. It was yet another Christmas without the gift I wanted most. In the evening, I was carefully examining the packages under the tree, pretending that I was merely rearranging them, when I suddenly spied a new, small package that was most intriguing. It was a blue Tiffany & Co. box! My husband had given me jewelry before, but never from Tiffany's. My mood was considerably lifted.

After dinner, my husband and I sat down next to the tree. I immediately chose the blue box I had spied earlier. He smiled tolerantly. When I opened it, there was a gold necklace with the word "MOM" as the pendant. Oh, no! The last thing I needed was to be reminded that we were still without a child. I kept my eyes down for a moment, hoping my husband would not see my misery and disappointment.

When I looked up, he was holding a packet of papers in front of his chest. The first page was a picture of a beautiful little girl from China! It quickly dawned on me that, somehow, he had received "the call" instead of me! This WAS my match presentation!

I pulled myself to my knees and thrust forward, hugging my husband and knocking him over in the process. We lay there on the floor, laughing and crying for quite a while as he explained that not only had he received the match call, but somewhere in the other packages was the ring that had originally come in that little blue box. It was the best Christmas ever... until the next year, when our daughter was home with us!

Tie a Ribbon

When I was a teen, there was a song out about tying a yellow ribbon around the old oak tree. This became symbolic for people waiting for someone to come home, especially in military families like mine. Later, the whole symbolism was miniaturized. Today, you can see looped ribbon pins in varying colors for things like soldiers and breast cancer awareness. We would have liked to do that as people waiting for the adoption of our little girl, but the pink ribbon would have been misunderstood.

When the day finally came for our match call, my husband knew I was very, very anxious, but he encouraged me to go to work anyway. It would keep my mind off of things and since everybody knew about the adoption, it might be fun to share the big moment – as long as I conferenced him in, too.

At 11:51 a.m, the misery of several years of waiting came to an end when I heard the agency representative say those magic words, "This is your match call!" I asked her to hold while we tried to conference my husband in, but there was no answer at his office. We next tried to conference direct to his cell phone but that didn't work either. I even had the representative try it from her end. Nothing. I debated with myself for all about 10 seconds before I decided that my husband would just have to get the information from me!

I learned my little girl was just eight months old. She was in a southern province and was in foster care. The information about her height and weight seemed odd to me. Either those numbers were way off or we were bringing home a future participant in women's basketball! The emailed photo was Just. So. Beautiful. It was all incredibly wonderful. To be honest, I kind of forgot about my husband!

As I hung up, the office erupted into applause. For the next hour, everybody came to my cubicle oohing and aahing and asking questions. I kept trying to reach my husband. By then, I was getting a little concerned. Finally, my boss came over and told me that not only was I not getting any work done, neither was anybody else, so she congratulated me and gave me the rest of the day off. Because I was concerned about my husband, I drove first to his office, but he wasn't there. I tried his cell again but he didn't answer, so I headed home.

As I rounded the corner to our street, it became obvious. That morning, he waited until I went to work. He then tied about 50 gigantic pink ribbons in the front yard's oak tree. When I pulled in the driveway that afternoon, he was sitting on the front porch with champagne. He told me later he really didn't care what pink ribbons had come to symbolize nationwide, he knew what they meant to us.

Those pink ribbons stayed in the tree until our daughter was home for a few weeks. She played happily in her playpen, watching her daddy as he brought out the ladder and took the ribbons down. That day, we took a picture of her sitting on top of a veritable mountain of pink ribbons. It's now the portrait that hangs above our living room fireplace. It will likely be my favorite picture forever.

Breathless

I have been involved in marathons since I was in my early twenties. I've completed several, including Boston, more than once. I often tell people that running for 26 miles is nothing compared to the international adoption process!

As part of my daily routine, I get up early each morning and run seven miles. On the days that I work from home, I sometimes do an additional run at lunch time. In both cases, I usually have my phone with me, but I am listening to music through the headphones.

During one of my noon runs, I received a phone call. I could clearly see the agency name on the screen. I knew that matches were due, so I quickly answered with a breathless "Hello!"

As winded as I was from the run, it was nothing compared to the way the breath was knocked out of me when the agency representative congratulated me and said that she was looking at a picture of a darling little girl. MY little girl! I had so many questions but all I had was the phone to take down information. The situation quickly became both comical and frustrating as I asked a question, told her to hold on, typed the response into the "note" then switched back to the phone call. After about 20 rounds of this, I finally felt like I had all the information I would need to relay to my husband. She told me that she was emailing me the picture. She waited until I was able to pull it up on the phone. Once again, I found I could hardly breathe. She was *stunning!*

For a few minutes, I just stood there trying to let it all sink in. I realized I needed to call my husband. I debated waiting until I got home, where I wouldn't have to go through the crazy machinations of switching from phone notes to phone call and back, but decided the frustration was worth it. And it was! Not that he would ever admit it, but with every tidbit of information I gave him, he would gasp and have to take a few seconds before he could respond. I knew he had to do that to keep from crying.

When the email came through to him, all I heard was, "Oh, my!" followed by more gasping. After what seemed like five minutes, he finally said, "She takes my breath away!"

She still does.

An unexpected Match

When we started our adoption, we thought the whole thing would take about three years. We were so naive! After waiting more than five years, we started to think about quitting, but several of our friends had chosen to leave the traditional program and were now happily home with children from the special needs program. We felt like we should at least explore that as an option.

We talked to several parents and talked to the agency representatives in the special needs programs. We even interviewed a few doctors about the various special needs. The more we learned, the more comfortable we became.

Eventually, we got around to submitting the checklist, but were warned that because we had very, very narrow ranges on everything from age to condition, we were probably looking at about one more year until they would be able to find files for us to review. Another year? That would put us at nearly seven years for our adoption. *Seven years?* That was the same amount of time that the domestic agency had told us and was one of the reasons why we had chosen to go with an international adoption instead. We were so discouraged.

Several months passed before the phone rang and we saw that it was the agency. It was exciting to know that they had found a file for us before an entire year had passed. We picked up the phone and the agency representative told us she was looking at a picture of our daughter. We were so excited! We learned her age, location, and even the meaning of her Chinese name.

"What is her special need?" we asked nervously. This all sounded wonderful, but if her special need was something we were not prepared to handle, it was going to crush us.

"What?" came the reply. "Did you request a certain special need?" Well, of course we did. Was the woman crazy? We had turned in a very specific checklist months ago and told her this.

"Let me start again," she said. "This is your match call. You have been matched with a healthy little girl. She does not have any special needs."

It turned out that even though we had submitted a checklist, it didn't have any affect on our dossier in the traditional program. The timing had just worked out so that we received our original match before the agency was able to locate a special needs child for us. It didn't matter. We were just so happy to finally have our child. It took a few more minutes and a lot further explanation, but we were finally all having the same conversation. Our unexpected Match Day turned out to be the best day of our lives – because that was the day we became a family.

COUNTRY GIRL

After waiting for almost double the amount of years we thought we would, it was finally our Match Day! The agency had let everyone know that the matches were in and being translated. I knew we would get "the call" some time that day, but had no idea if it would be in the morning, afternoon, or into the night.

We don't have cell phones because they won't work out here in the boonies. I was not at all sure I wanted to leave home since the house phone was the only way our agency could contact me. My husband, Dan, seemed to sympathize, but he pointed out that even if it was going to be the most exciting day of our lives, there were chores to do and errands to run. "We have to take our chances," he said. Seeing my face, he continued with a gentle tongue-in-cheek ribbing, "Now, come on, Bessie, you know those chickens need feeding and the cow needs milking. The animals aren't gonna wait."

"Bessie is the cow's name, not mine!" I retorted. Usually, I enjoyed the way Dan poked fun at our rural lifestyle. A lot of our city friends had gently ribbed us about moving out into the country and "going organic" but we actually had a long-term business plan. We knew eventually we would be selling our products to high-end grocery stores in the city we had left behind.

Today, I wasn't in the mood for jokes or work. I just wanted to get the errands done as quickly as possible so I could be there when "the call" came in. I ran by the tack store for the horse supplement we needed and then I picked up some barbed wire my husband had ordered. Pushing the unwieldy roll into the bed of the pickup, I caught a glimpse of myself in a store window. It wasn't a joke! In my leather gloves, jeans, plaid shirt and beat-up straw cowboy hat, I exemplified the rural life. I didn't just look like the farmer's wife, I now looked like the farmer!

As soon as I hit the door at home, I checked for voicemail. There wasn't anything, so I got back into the truck and drove to where I knew Dan was working with the soy that morning. When he saw me, it was obvious he thought I was there to tell him about the match. I felt so guilty.

I tried to explain about seeing myself in the window. I was talking quickly and crying. I'm sure I sounded like I had lost my mind, we have been married a long time, and he knows me well.

"Come with me," he commanded. We got into his truck and he drove me back to the house, where he instructed me to go take a bath in the upstairs bathroom, and to put on some nice clothes. "You know," he said, "from the old life."

The bath was just what I needed. After an hour or so, I came floating back down the stairs, squeaky clean, with a little makeup on, wearing one of my favorite dresses. I found Dan waiting for me in the dining room in a suit. He had made us a terrific pasta salad and he served wine. It was an elegant, relaxing meal.

We were dressed to the nines, well fed, and happy. When "the call" came, it was the best dessert ever! That's how the tradition of once-a-week dress up meals began in our little farmhouse. Our daughter hates them. She is growing up to be a country cowgirl through and through.

HOW DOES YOUR GARDEN GROW?

We knew we were going to be in the next round of matches. Trying to tell myself that it would be at least a month and maybe longer wasn't working out too well. I was a mess!

One of the ways I handle stress is to get out in my garden. There's just something about handling the dirt, getting the seeds planted at just the right depth, and working to keep everything pest and disease free that suits me. I'm that rare breed that actually enjoys weeding!

During the weeks before our match I was in the garden every single day. There wasn't a weed left. I planted vegetables I'd never even heard of before, worked with the bulbs I had rooted the previous fall – anything to keep me moving, so I wouldn't worry about when the match was coming.

The day "the call" came in, I was on my hands and knees digging the wells for the new border of trees that I had, in my nervous energy, decided was absolutely necessary. This was not just a border for the garden. It extended along one entire side of our back yard, which meant there was a lot of measuring in order to get it just right. I needed the plants to grow in a straight line, so I literally had to lie down on the ground to get the proper line of sight. It was a very dirty job.

My husband tried to hand me the phone, but my gloves (not to mention pretty much the rest of me) were caked with mud, so he held the phone up to my ear. It was quite a sight. He was trying not to step in the mud so he was leaning at a precarious angle. I was already covered with mud. When I started crying, my tears of joy were watery streaks of dirt running down my cheeks. My husband toppled over, and the two of us ended up sitting in the mud together during the phone call that would change our lives!

What I didn't realize was that before bringing the phone to me, my husband had arranged for our son to video the entire episode. We sometimes watch that video, even now after nearly three years. Our daughter, who is very much a fastidious girly-girl type, loves to comment, "Ooooh, Mommy! You yucky muddy!" She still won't help me in the garden!

Whisper on the Wind

Both of us are in the medical field, so when we decided to adopt a special needs child we felt well prepared. We knew that whatever the situation, if we couldn't figure it out for ourselves, we had hundreds of professionals we could turn to for any needed help. We began looking by going to the usual websites. We found that there were kids we thought we could manage but we wanted to feel we were drawn to a specific child.

My husband decided we should go ahead and choose an agency so that we could get files sent to us. One agency explained that the children listed online were a very small percentage of the files they were receiving; another told us that because we were open to so many conditions, once we completed a dossier, it would not be very long before we would be matched. It seemed to us that it would take about a year, and that seemed reasonable.

We finished our agency application and medical conditions list and sent it to the agency. They let us know they received it on a Wednesday. We received a nice explanation that once we finished that step, because we had included a broad range of acceptable special needs, it would be a matter of months, possibly even just weeks, before we would begin seeing files for a possible match.

On Friday evening, just two days after the agency received our application, we received "the call" from them, saying they had a possible match. We were stunned, but really excited! We told them to send the file.

Unfortunately, my husband received an emergency call and had to leave, but he told me to go ahead and see what I thought of the file. The sweet little face that stared out at me from our computer screen just about broke my heart. This was a beautiful child, but her eyes looked sad and blank. I was as concerned for her emotional condition as I was for her medical condition. Wanting to really examine the file thoroughly with no distractions, I made myself a cup of coffee and headed for our back porch. The sunshine, the views, and the winds in the pines are calming to me, so I often go there for what I call natural sustenance.

She had a pretty serious situation. From my medical training, I knew that without intervention, she was likely to have a very abbreviated lifespan. Even with treatment, she was bound to have a medically challenged life. I closed my eyes for a minute in order to clear my mind, but bolted upright when I heard somebody whisper to me!

I am a scientist. I do *not* hear voices, see ghosts, or catch whispers on the wind. But that morning I *know* I heard, "Go quickly."

My husband found my revelation a little strange, but after he examined the file, he agreed she would be a good fit for us. It was still many, many months until we traveled to meet our daughter. It didn't seem nearly fast enough to me. When we arrived, she was very ill. She ended up needing emergency surgery not long after we arrived home. The timing turned out to be critical. These days, she often sits on the back porch with me and asks if I can hear the wind whispering. I tell her Yes. Every. Time.

OUR thanks

The authors wish to express their sincere, heartfelt appreciation and gratitude to the families who contributed to the creation of this book.

We are humbled by your willingness to share such a personal story with others, and deeply touched by your ability to love a child halfway around the world you've never met.

To order print or reader copies
of this book, please visit

http://www.marcinsonpress.com
or
http://www.amazon.com.

Made in the USA
San Bernardino, CA
01 November 2013